KALAMAZOO COUNTY
CHARACTERS

KALAMAZOO COUNTY
CHARACTERS

DIANNA HIGGS STAMPFLER

THE
History
PRESS

Published by The History Press
Charleston, SC
www.historypress.com

Copyright © 2025 by Dianna Stampfler
All rights reserved

First published 2025

Manufactured in the United States

ISBN 9781467155922

Library of Congress Control Number: 2024945423

For my father, whose Kalamazoo story is and forever will be my favorite to tell.

CONTENTS

PREFACE

I took my first breath in Kalamazoo, at Bronson Hospital. My birth certificate is proof: 3:15 p.m. on May 30, 1969—it was a Friday. My arrival may have pleased my parents, but I suspect my older brother was less than enthused, as not only was I born on his fifth birthday, but in doing so, I also forced the postponement or perhaps the cancellation of his party with friends.

My family lived twelve miles north of Kalamazoo in the small town of Plainwell (1970 census: 3,195 | 2020 census: 3,933), where my granddaughters will hopefully be the fifth generation on my paternal side to attend Plainwell Community Schools (and the fourth through Gilkey Elementary). Up until his passing on May 5, 2024, my dad still lived there, in the house where his mother was raised and where we moved to when I was six years old.

While Plainwell had a small downtown business district, "the strip" along M-89 between Plainwell and Otsego (just west of US-131) had yet to transform into the big box store haven that it is today. When we needed to shop for school clothes or supplies, we went to Kalamazoo. Holiday catalogs from Sears, JCPenney, Montgomery Ward and Witmark gave us reasons to dream, but usually, shopping was done in person at these stores.

For most of my early childhood, my dad worked in Kalamazoo as a DJ (disc jockey) at WKMI, the hottest AM music radio station in West Michigan at the time (see pages 134–137). Sometimes, we would stop by and see him when we were in the area, and even four decades later, I can still see the station vividly in my memory: his office with the posters of rock stars on the wall, the jukebox in the lobby where we played the Beatles' "Yellow Submarine," the news teletype room that was overflowing with paper, the glass Coke bottle machine in the basement and the inground swimming pool in the backyard. It broke my heart when I heard, years later, that the new station owners filled that pool in with concrete. I have so many great memories of Saturdays swimming and eating olive loaf sandwiches, washing them down with Mr. Pibb (the poor man's version of Dr Pepper).

For as long as I can remember, my mom's side of the family has gathered for Easter brunch—a tradition started by my grandparents when I was young. As the family grew—I am the third oldest of a dozen cousins, and my mom is the oldest of five children—we found the only restaurants that could accommodate our large group were in Kalamazoo County. Iconic buffet eateries like Sveden House, The Stagecoach and Holly's are all gone now, but thankfully, we have memories and lots of photos. We still gather, and with blended families and four generations, we can top out at over seventy some years.

I was just shy of eleven on Tuesday, May 13, 1980, when an F3 tornado ripped through downtown Kalamazoo. Five people were killed that day, and seventy-nine were injured. As the twister spent sixteen minutes on the ground and traveled eleven miles, it left behind over $50 million in damages. While I was home at the time, my sixteen-year-old brother was playing high school JV baseball against Hacket Catholic at Sutherland Field (currently the home of the Kalamazoo Growlers on Kings Highway near downtown), and I remember hearing stories about the players taking cover in the dugouts and the field being trashed with debris afterward.

When I was a teenager, Kalamazoo was a social hub. We walked countless steps at Maple Hill Mall, stopping to replenish at Orange Julius, Hot Sam, TE Murch's or Sbarro Pizza. Across the road, West Main Mall had dwindled to nothing more than a movie theater and an arcade, perfect for group hangouts or casual dates. Even our senior prom was held in Kalamazoo, on the historic campus of Nazareth College (see related stories on pages 72–73 "Sisters of St. Joseph" and 94–95 "Lavern Harman"), which was razed just a few years ago.

After graduating from Plainwell High School in 1987, I became a commuter student at Western Michigan University (WMU) in Kalamazoo, where I majored in English and communications (print and broadcast journalism). One of my noted teachers was Tom Bailey, who introduced me to Michigan author Sue Hubbell (see pages 96–97). Just recently, I uncovered several papers I wrote for his class, including a review of Hubbell's memoir, *A Country Year, Living the Questions*.

While at WMU, I was active in several student organizations and worked a handful of jobs, including serving as a copy editor for the *Western Herald* student newspaper. While coming home one night, driving north along US-131 near D Avenue, after putting the paper to bed, I witnessed a strange occurrence in the sky. Faint tones of greens and yellows danced above the horizon in some bizarre space show. Years would pass before I realized that what I had observed was the illusive Aurora Borealis (Northern Lights). I've seen them only twice since (on March 17, 2015, and March 23, 2023, both "Up North").

For a brief period, between 1991 and 1993, I lived in Schoolcraft, and on July 30, 1992, my daughter was born at Borgess Hospital (see pages 72–73), making me a mother. My great-grandmother (my daughter's great-great-grandmother) was in the same hospital at the same time, and we were able to get the only photo of them together on the day I was released. My great-grandmother died less than two weeks later. In February 2020 and October 2023, my granddaughters (my son's daughters) were also born at Borgess.

One of the most exciting Kalamazoo experiences came in the spring of 2006. Having launched my marketing company, Promote Michigan, two years prior, I was actively acquiring new clients and projects to make ends meet as a single mother. I can't remember exactly how I was connected, but soon, I was meeting with sisters and producers Joanna Clare Scott and Dana Kowalski, along with director David O'Malley, planning the promotion of the film *Kalamazoo?* I was responsible for finding sponsors for a media bus trip to about a half-dozen film sites, including Sweetwater Donuts, Bell's Brewery, Food Dance Café and the Kalamazoo Civic Theatre, as well as planning the red carpet premiere with celebrities Mayim Bialik, Josie Davis, Chita Rivera and Michael Boatman. Somewhere, I still have a DVD copy of the film and an autographed copy of a film poster as a reminder.

On October 9, 2015, my extended family gathered at the historic Henderson Castle in downtown Kalamazoo to celebrate my dad's seventy-first birthday. After taking a tour (along with pictures from the roof of this regal abode), we sat down to a gut-gorging six-course meal prepared by owner/chef François Louis Moyet. The location was purposefully selected, as my dad had never been in the castle, even though he was (we are) distantly related to its original owners. Frank Henderson (see pages 74–75) built this majestic home for his wife, Mary Taylor, who was my dad's first cousin four times removed. Her uncle Alexander was my dad's great-great-great-grandfather (on his mother's side).

Ten years ago, I moved "Up North," and now my trips to Kalamazoo aren't as frequent. Yet in preparing for this book, I returned several times in 2023 to do research or grab photos. While in town in January 2023, I was taken on a tour of Heritage Guitar, the historic building which once housed Gibson Guitars (see pages 34–35). In August, I attended the unveiling of an Abraham Lincoln statue in Bronson Park (see pages 56–57), followed by a rural road trip in search of the stone structures built by Laverne Harman (see pages 94–95). In late November, I stopped by WMU to carefully flip through century-old court records at the Zhang Legacy Collections Center related to the case of Etta Fairchild (see pages 80–81), followed by a ceremony at the Alumni Center inside Heritage Hall, built in part by Albert White (see pages 36–37).

Choosing the fifty figures to feature in this book was not an easy task—my original list had over one hundred names on it. In some instances, I made a last-minute decision to select a family member because I found their story equally compelling—such was the case with Uriah Upjohn (see pages 70–71) and Ted Nowak (see pages 106–107). Many I have personal connections with, as I have told their stories in other formats before, and it was exciting to dig in even deeper to look for lesser-known facts. One profile isn't even a person at all, but an award-winning horse named Temple Flora (see pages 104–105). In order to showcase as many individuals as possible, I limited each profile to two pages (approximately 650 words) with one photograph—the exception being the last write-up about my dad, my favorite Kalamazoo story to tell.

ACKNOWLEDGEMENTS

Much of my research was done online, using sites such as Newspapers. com, NewsBank.com, FindAGrave.com, Ancestry.com, FamilySearch. org and both the "Vanished Kalamazoo" and "You know you're from Plainwell if you remember…" groups on Facebook, among others.

A handful of individuals assisted me in verifying information, securing photos and connecting with sources, including Lynne Houghton and John Winchell, Zhang Legacy Collections Center at Western Michigan University; Ryan Gage, Kalamazoo Public Library; Regina Gorham, Kalamazoo Valley Museum; Roberto Lara and Amy Ferguson, The Fetzer Institute; Sandy Stamm and Julie Stout, Ransom District Library in Plainwell; Teresa Stannard and Karen Woodworth, Parchment Community Library; Cheryl H. Lyon-Jenness, Western Michigan University; Kayla Miller, Portage Public Schools; Lisa Gibbon and Sarah Lubelski, Congregation of St. Joseph; Holly Stephenson, St. Joseph County Historical Society; Fred Burwell, Beloit College; Colleen Lies, Wisconsin Historical Foundation; Harmony J. Miller, Nottawa Township Library; Rosemary LaDuke, Kalamazoo Garden Council; Lisa Murphy, Kalamazoo College; Mary K. Huelsbeck, Wisconsin Center for Film and Theater Research; Sue Bullard, Milford Historical Society; Brendan and Penelope Alex Ragotzy, The Barn Theatre School; and Nikki Statler, Air Zoo; as well as Don Parfet, Mary Becktell, Brian and Liddy Hubbell, Judy Berger, Diana Curtis, Julie Gilbert, Mary Duncan, Sherry VanDam, Larry Bell, Sharon and Mike Nicholson. I also appreciate the support of my colleagues and friends at Discover Kalamazoo and the Radisson Plaza Hotel at Kalamazoo Center.

A special thank-you to my dad, Jim Higgs, who proofread every profile and offered input on the order of the sections and even suggested some of the individuals to be featured. It is his passion for history and, specifically, his own Kalamazoo story (see pages 134–137) that led to the writing of this book.

INTRODUCTION

The first inhabitants in what became Kalamazoo were "moundbuilders" who lived here at least three hundred years ago, and one of their best-known remnants in the county is found in Bronson Park. The flowing river, referred to as "Kekalamasoe" or "Kalamasoe" (thought to mean "boiling pot," "mirage," and/or "reflecting river") drew early traders, including Gurdon Saltonstall Hubbard, who noted in a letter that he spent the winter of 1820–21 at a post built by a man named Laframboin. Another noted trader, both here and around Michigan, was Rix Robinson, who had an outpost near the present-day Paterson Street Bridge. Missionaries came next, including the Reverend Leonard Slater, who died here in 1866 and was buried in Riverside Cemetery.

Much of what is now the city of Kalamazoo, along the Kalamazoo River, was part of a Pottawatomi Reservation called Match-E-Be-Nash-She-Wish, established by the Treaty of Chicago in 1821. The land was reclaimed by the U.S. government six years later and the Natives were forced out around 1840. In April 2019, a series of street signs identifying the nine-square-mile reservation's original boundaries were installed at intersections on Riverview Drive, Patterson and Whites Roads and several other noted intersections around town as part of an initiative by the Kalamazoo Reservation Public Education Committee.

But what about the four other jurisdictions in the United States that are called Kalamazoo—an unincorporated area in Logan County, Arkansas; an unincorporated community in southwest Volusia County, now a privately owned, in Florida; an unincorporated community in Madison County, Nebraska; and an unincorporated community in Barbour County, West Virginia? Where did they come up with the name?

Kalamazoo County was organized on July 3, 1830, by an act of the territorial legislature and approved by Territorial Governor Lewis Cass (who served in that role from 1813 to 1831). The next year, the area's first permanent white settler, Titus Bronson, recorded his plat at the County Register of Deeds Office and proudly proclaimed the community named Bronson. In 1836, disgruntled residents forced him out of his town and changed its name to Kalamazoo, which now refers to a city, county, river and college.

There are several institutes of higher learning in Kalamazoo that have educated thousands over the years, including several well-known people. Founded in 1833 as the Michigan and Huron Institute, today's Kalamazoo College is the oldest private college and one of the oldest overall colleges or universities in the nation. Western State Normal School was founded in 1903, becoming Western Michigan University in 1957. Kalamazoo Valley Community College was founded in 1966.

One of the earliest associations formed to promote business in town was the Kalamazoo Regional Chamber of Commerce, founded in 1903. In the fall of 1974, Richard Caroll was hired as the first executive director of the newly organized Kalamazoo County Convention and Visitors Bureau (branded today as Discover Kalamazoo, DiscoverKalamazoo.com). By the following August, he had resigned, and Diane Smusz took the helm. It was about this time that the city's still-popular slogan was born: "Yes, There Really Is a Kalamazoo." This was a response, likely, to that Glenn Miller song. There were buttons, T-shirts and bumper stickers emblazoned with this message. It was revised slightly after the tornado in May 1980 to "Yes, There Really Still Is a Kalamazoo."

Kalamazoo is featured in several well-known and obscure books, poems and songs dating to the nineteenth century:

- L. Frank Baum (author of *The Wizard of Oz* who coincidentally spent his summers in nearby Holland) penned a short verse in 1899 about a boy from Kalamazoo who ate too much hot celery stew, which appeared in his book *Father Goose*. A nice nod to the agricultural commodity brought to the area by Scotsman George Taylor (see pages 40–41).

- American poet Vachel Lindsay, considered the founder of modern singing poetry, published his 367-word poem "Kalamazoo" in August 1919.
- Three-time Pulitzer Prize–winning writer Carl Sandburg (who spent his summers near Harbert, Michigan, in Berrien County) published an 890-word poem called "The Sins of Kalamazoo" in 1927 (that title recirculated in 2019 as a true crime book about the unsolved murder of a Kalamazoo man, Louis Schilling, written by J. Thomas Buttery).
- Kalamazoo is mentioned in the children's book *Horton Hatches the Egg*, written and illustrated by Theodor Geisel under the pseudonym Dr. Seuss, published by Random House in 1940.
- One of the most notable references is in the song "I've Got a Gal in Kalamazoo," by Glenn Miller. It was the best-selling record in 1942, spending multiple weeks at number 1 on the charts.
- *The Train to Timbucktoo*, by Margarete Wise Brown, with pictures by Art Seiden, was originally published as a Little Golden Book in 1951 and tells the story of trains big and small traveling between Timbucktoo and Kalamazoo.
- In 1953, Warner Brothers and Western Publishing Company released a thirty-nine-cent book called *TWEETY*, and its first line reads, "In a very small city near Kalamazoo…"
- In 1969, Credence Clearwater Revival released their fourth studio album, *Willy and the Poor Boys*, and the single "Down on the Corner" references Kalamazoo in relation to a Gibson guitar (see pages 34–35). Other songs referencing the city include: "I've Been Everywhere" by Hank Snow (1962); "Turnpike Tom" by Steve Goodman (1971); "Mary Lou" by Bob Seger (1976); "Della and the Dealer" by Hoyt Axton (1979); "Jumbo Go Away" by Frank Zappa (1981); "Kalamazoo" by Primus (1997); "Kalamazoo" by Ben Folds (2004); "I Can't Stand L.A." by Bowling for Soup (2009); "Gotta Get Away" by The Black Keys (2014); and "Kalamazoo" by The Show Ponies (2017).
- Michigan author Johnathan Rand added *Kreepy Klowns of Kalamazoo* to his Michigan Chiller series of children's books in 2000.

Since Kalamazoo's founding, eleven presidents and/or presidential candidates have visited, according to a 2021 story on WWMT.com. These visitors included: Abraham Lincoln, August 27, 1856 (see pages 56–57); William McKinley, October 1899; Theodore Roosevelt, September 8, 1900; William Howard Taft, September 1911 and September 1921; Dwight D. Eisenhower, October 1952; John F. Kennedy, October 1960; Richard Nixon, 1952, 1956, 1958 and October 27, 1960; Gerald R. Ford (the only U.S. president from Michigan), early 1974; Bill Clinton, August 1996; George W. Bush, 2000, 2001 and 2004; Barack Obama, June 10, 2010; Joe Biden, February 19, 2021.

Kalamazoo County is home to four cities, five villages and fifteen townships (see next page). It also has three sister cities: Numazu, Japan; Kingston, Jamaica; and Pushkin, Russia.

KALAMAZOO COUNTY

CITIES

Galesburg

Kalamazoo (county seat)

Parchment

Portage

VILLAGES

Augusta

Climax

Richland

Schoolcraft

Vicksburg

TOWNSHIPS

Alamo

Brady

Charleston

Climax

Comstock

Cooper

Kalamazoo

Oshtemo

Pavilion

Prairie Ronde

Richland

Ross

Schoolcraft

Texas

Wakeshma

SECTION 1
EARLY PIONEERS

DELAMORE DUNCAN

Several firsts in Kalamazoo County history can be attributed to one family (primarily a father and son), who made the treacherous journey from the East Coast to the Territory of Michigan in the mid-1820s.

A native of Lyman, New Hampshire, and of Irish-Scottish descent, Delamore Duncan was born on November 24, 1805, to William and Ruth (Gilmore) Duncan. William was a prominent citizen in Grafton County, even teaching at the common school in nearby Monroe, where Delamore was enrolled at the age of five. His mother died in 1821, when Delamore was just sixteen; his father would go on to marry three more times.

There are more than fifty mentions of Delamore Duncan in *The History of Kalamazoo County, Michigan* (Samuel W. Durant, 1880), including a detailed biographical sketch. From this record, it is known that in April 1825, the father and son started out for the Michigan Territory, traveling via the recently completed Erie Canal to Buffalo, New York, and then taking a steamer to Detroit. They spent a little time in Washtenaw County and then moved around the Great Lakes region, primarily in Ohio.

In February 1829, Delamore hitched his ox team to his wagon and again navigated toward Michigan, arriving in Prairie Ronde, where he selected a desired parcel of land on which to build a future home. He soon returned to Ohio to work and, on September 8, married Parmela Clark in Lyme Township. They went on to have nine biological children—five of whom died of scarlet fever—and are also credited with raising no less than sixteen other children.

Delamore joined his father, stepmother and three siblings on their trip to Prairie Ronde in October 1829, where the patriarch had erected a sixteen-by-twenty-four-foot log home. As the abode was not quite fit for

DELLAMORE H. DUNCAN.

From the History of Kalamazoo County *(1880).*

occupancy, the family moved in temporarily with Colonel Abiel Fellows. The next April, the Duncan men constructed a twenty-by-twenty-four-foot granary on their property, three and a half miles west of present-day Schoolcraft, said to be the first frame building in the county and home to regular justice court sessions.

That October, Delamore walked from Prairie Ronde back to Ohio to secure money to purchase land, returning home in twelve days. It took some time, but he eventually erected a frame house, which he called home for the remainder of his life (said to be the first frame house in Kalamazoo County), located west of Eleventh Street and north of XY Avenue.

Delamore was an esteemed member of his community. He was elected the first sheriff of Kalamazoo County, serving from 1830 to 1834 and using his home as the jail until a county facility was built. He served nine years as township supervisor and even more as justice of the peace, although he never had to settle a lawsuit, as his mediation skills brought resolution before a trial was needed.

He was a founding trustee of Kalamazoo College in 1833, served as an inspector for the Prairie Ronde Township Schools and was a leader of the underground railroad in western Michigan. He was a stockholder in the Kalamazoo and Three Rivers Plank-Road Company, which laid the first real thoroughfare between Kalamazoo and Schoolcraft in the 1850s. Delamore was also a president of the Schoolcraft and Three Rivers Railroad Company and was an organizer of the First National Bank of Three Rivers, serving as a director for six years.

Delamore was elected to the Michigan House of Representatives on November 5, 1849 (sworn in on January 7, 1850). Formerly a member of the Whig and Free Soil Parties, he joined the Republican Party and was a delegate to the first convention on July 6, 1854, in Jackson, Michigan. He was also a member of the Constitutional Convention in 1867.

Delamore Duncan died on May 1, 1870, at the age of sixty-four and was buried in the Harrison Cemetery in Schoolcraft, Michigan, next to Parmela, who died in 1891.

BAZEL HARRISON

One of the most prolific pioneer families in Kalamazoo County boasts more than one thousand descendants, all of whom can trace their ancestry back to one steadfast man.

Bazel Calvin Harrison was born on March 15, 1771, in Frederick County, Maryland, to William Henry and his second wife, Worlenda Jane (Davis) Harrison. William's brother was Benjamin Harrison, a signer of the Declaration of Independence, who, in turn, was the father of William Henry Harrison, the ninth president of the United States (who died just thirty-one days after his inauguration in 1841, making his the shortest presidency in U.S. history).

As a child, Bazel lived with his family in Virginia and, later, Pennsylvania. On March 17, 1790, just two days after his nineteenth birthday, Bazel eloped with seventeen-year-old Martha Jane Stillwell, much to the admonition of her mother (and approval of her father, a witness to the union). Ten months later, to the date, the couple welcomed the first of their seventeen children (Bazel himself was one of twenty-three children born to his father and his two wives).

After years of living in Pennsylvania, Kentucky and Ohio, Bazel and Martha decided to move to the territory of Michigan. Sometime in September 1828, they set out with eight of their children, a handful of grandchildren and some neighbors for the two-month trek northwest. Bazel was fifty-seven years old at the time.

A biographical sketch of Bazel was published in the weekly *Kalamazoo Telegraph* in 1874, including an account of the group's arrival on the outskirts of present-day Schoolcraft: "On the evening of the 5th day of November, 1828, just at dusk, they lighted their camp-fires on the southwestern edge of Prairie Ronde, or *Wa-we-os-co-tung-sco-tah*, as the Indians called it, meaning

Schoolcraft Historical Society and Museum.

the 'round-fire plain,' whence comes the French 'Prairie Ronde.'"

Among the first to welcome the weary travelers was Pottawatomie chief Sagamaw, along with a dozen of his braves. Bazel was able to communicate with the chief and determined a suitable location to settle—along the northwest side of a small nearby lake (since named Harrison's Lake). The family acquired land from the office in Monroe and erected a cabin to get them through that first winter. In doing so, they became the first permanent settlers in the area.

The next year, the land was divided, and a community emerged. Around 1831–32, Bazel built the first frame house in the county, where he lived until his death. Then his youngest son, John, lived in the homestead until his passing in 1908. Owen, John's youngest, moved into the house next. An article about a Harrison family reunion published on July 10, 1927, in the *Kalamazoo Gazette* noted that the third-generation Owen was still living in the house.

Bazel earned the moniker "Judge Harrison" in 1831 after Michigan's territorial governor Lewis Cass named him one of the associate judges for Kalamazoo County. Although Bazel held the position only until 1834, he proudly retained the title; he later served as justice of the peace for the county. Bazel was a strong Democrat until he voted for Abraham Lincoln (see pages 56–57) in 1861. He was also a religious Methodist man, with an unusually strong, musical bass voice. Bazel also has the eternal distinction of being the inspiration for the character of Ben Boden (the Beekeeper) in author James Fenimore Cooper's book *Oak Openings* (see pages 84–85).

At the time of his death on August 30, 1874, Bazel was 103 years old—the oldest person in the county (perhaps the state)—and over one thousand people attended his funeral. "He had no disease, but had worn the thread of life completely out, and passed peacefully to rest," according to his obituary in the *Chicago Tribune*.

Bazel and Martha, along with two dozen other members of the family, are buried in the Harrison Cemetery in Schoolcraft. A historical marker about the family also stands nearby.

TITUS BRONSON

The first white settler to make his way to present-day Kalamazoo in 1829 was regarded as an eccentric man with a penchant for trouble, yet without his pioneering spirit, one could question when the area would have been founded and how its future would have played out.

Titus Bronson was born in Middlebury, Connecticut, on November 27, 1788, to Hannah (Cook) and Titus Bronson, a Revolutionary War veteran. At the age of thirty-three, the younger Titus moved to Tallmadge, Ohio, where he learned to grow seed potatoes (earning the moniker "Potato Bronson") and met the woman who would become his wife, Sarah Eliza Bartholomew. They were married on January 18, 1827, in Middlebury by Reverend Mark Mead. The couple had two children, William and Julia.

The enactment of the Land Act of 1820—which reduced the price of federal land within the Northwest Territory to $1.25 an acre, with a minimum purchase of eighty acres, along with a down payment of only $100 for property—along with the opening of the Erie Canal in 1825, resulted in a population influx into the Michigan Territory. According to the Detroit Historical Society, by the 1830s, Michigan had become the fastest growing territory in America.

Among those who took advantage of these expansion opportunities was Titus Bronson, who, between 1824 and 1839, amassed over 4,400 acres in Michigan through eighteen different transactions. In 1825, he was reportedly living in Huron River Township (Washtenaw County), and in late spring of 1829, he set out along an old wooded Native trail and arrived at what the Pottawatomi called the Kekalamasoe River, meaning "the mirage or reflecting river," on June 21 that year.

An article published in the June 27, 1909 issue of the *Detroit Free Press* references a letter that Titus had sent back east to his family, noting, "There

Kalamazoo Public Library.

is an ideal place for a home. I will settle there and then go back east after my relatives." He then used tamarack poles to construct a crude hut, where he lived through the fall, spending the winter with friends in nearby Prairie Ronde (present-day Schoolcraft).

Titus briefly returned to Ohio in the spring to gather his family, including his brother-in-law Stephen Richardson, and brought them to Michigan to establish a community in the newly formed Kalamazoo County, which had been organized on May 7, 1830. Titus and Stephen were soon at work purchasing large tracts of land and platting the Village of Bronson (not to be confused with the village of Bronson, originally named York, founded decades later in nearby Branch County) which was recorded at the county register of deeds office in March 1831. That same year, Bronson was named the Kalamazoo County seat, and by 1832, the first post office had been established.

Over the next few years, the ever-peculiar Titus continued down an unfavorable path, speaking out against intemperance and politics, being fined for stealing a cherry tree from another resident and wandering around in shoddy dress. It was likely these unsavory characteristics that led locals to rename the town Kalamazoo in 1836, a year before Michigan achieved statehood. It was incorporated as a village in 1843, and in 1884, a city charter was adopted.

Titus left the area after the name change, working his way through the Midwest to Illinois and Iowa, where he lost his fortune in a shady land deal. He then returned to his hometown, where he died on January 6, 1853, at the age of sixty-four. He was buried in the Middlebury Cemetery beneath a headstone that reads: "A Western Pioneer, Returned to Sleep with his Fathers."

Bronson's legacy remains evident around Kalamazoo, including at Bronson Park (officially named on December 5, 1876) and Bronson Hospital (renamed in 1907). A state historic marker was also erected in 1971 at the southeast corner of North Park Street and West Water Street, near where Titus built his log home.

ENOCH HARRIS

K alamazoo County's first farmer might be pleased to know that Michigan has grown into the second most agriculturally diverse state in the country, with an apple industry valued at over $700 million.

Enoch "Knuck" Harris was born to an unnamed enslaved mother on November 15, 1784, in Virginia, and according to an article in the December 21, 1902 issue of the *Kalamazoo Morning Gazette News*, his father was "a man who afterwards held the highest office within the gift of the people of the United States." There were four men from Virginia who later became president of the United States: George Washington (who was forty-two years old in 1784 but never fathered any biological children), Thomas Jefferson (thirty-one), James Madison (twenty-three) and James Monroe (sixteen). "It might be impossible to prove either the truth or falsity of this statement now, but the story is not a new one and has been handed down from father to son as one of the traditions of the Harris family," the article concluded.

After being raised in Pennsylvania, Enoch made his way through Ohio and was one of the founders of Mount Vernon—named after George Washington's plantation in Virginia—in 1805. One of his neighbors was a nurseryman, John Chapman, who planted orchards around the Great Lakes region and was known as Johnny Appleseed. Both men are mentioned in the 1862 book *History of Knox County, Ohio 1779–1862*, published by A. Banning Norton.

In 1812, Enoch met and married Deborah Brown, a mulatto woman who was born in Pennsylvania on May 1, 1783, to unknown or unnamed parents. The Harrises would go on to have ten children—five boys and five girls— eight of whom were born in Ohio.

Soon after his marriage, Enoch enlisted as a private in Captain James Rightmire's company during the War of 1812, serving from May 4 to May 19,

Kalamazoo Public Library.

1813, and again from September 8, 1814, to March 5, 1815, under Colonel Alexander Enos in the First Regiment of Ohio Militias.

After his service ended, Enoch moved his family around Ohio until they relocated to Michigan, showing up for the first time in the 1830 census. He settled on an eighty-acre parcel in Brady Township, and by June 20, 1831, he had purchased land in sections 35 and 36 in Genesee Prairie (at the crossroads of Parkview and Eleventh Streets in present-day Oshtemo Township). There were only a handful of residents in Kalamazoo County at the time, but Enoch soon built a family cabin and began tilling the land as the county's first farmer. He also planted the county's first apple tree, and descendants speculate whether the seeds came from his former Mount Vernon neighbor.

According to the 1840 census, the Harrises were the only Black family in Oshtemo Township (which had been founded in 1839), and Enoch was looking into new opportunities. His name appeared on the ballot for the Fifth Senatorial District during a special election on December 31, 1841. Out of thirteen candidates, he came in third place with 85 votes—George Redfield won, with 267 votes, followed by John P. Marsh with 132.

His political career behind him, Enoch returned his focus to farming. In 1850, his operation was valued at $4,000, and ten years later that number doubled. The 1860 agricultural census noted that he had nearly 150 acres of land, owned horses and dairy cows and grew a variety of grains. He eventually owned over 200 acres. Described as an honest old man, Enoch was known to have cordial relationships with most members of the community and often settled land disputes as they developed among his neighbors.

Enoch died of kidney disease at the age of eighty-five, on March 21, 1870. Deborah died on May 2, 1881, and both were buried in the Genesee Prairie Cemetery, where a historical marker was erected in 1973. The Harris home, which stood at 5821 Parkview Street, adjacent to the cemetery, was torn down in 2006 after years of abandonment and neglect.

SECTION 2

INNOVATORS, GROUNDBREAKERS AND ENTREPRENEURS

ORVILLE H. GIBSON

One of the world's most iconic musical instrument brands got its humble beginnings in downtown Kalamazoo, founded by an innovative man with a creative bent and lofty dreams.

The youngest of John W. and Amy (Nichols) Gibson's five children, Orville H. was born in May 1856 in Franklin County, New York. Around the age of nineteen, Orville—already a noted musician and performer—joined his older brother Lovell in the Kalamazoo area.

According to the Kalamazoo Public Library website (KPL.gov), Gibson performed with the Young Men's Organ Association of the First Presbyterian Church in April 1876 and was known to stroll the streets entertaining crowds. Later that summer, he joined the Michigan State Troops as a musician in Company C of the Second Infantry Regiment and was stationed at Camp Custer, at that time located near Grand Rapids. Orville remained with the group through at least August 1879, racking up marksman accolades during unit target shooting contests.

Returning to Kalamazoo in 1880, Orville worked as a shoe store clerk by day and honed his musical skills in his free time. He even formed the "Young Men's Musician Minstrels" with local entertainers, performing in at least forty shows on the guitar, mandolin and banjo, in both solo and ensemble acts.

A skilled luthier (a craftsperson who specializes in string instruments that have a neck and sound box), Orville also began designing musical instruments. In December 1891, he left his shoe store job to devote more time to his hobby, and in 1894, at the age of thirty-eight, he founded the Gibson Mandolin-Guitar Manufacturing Co.

The next May, Orville applied for a patent for an "improved mandolin," which was awarded no. 598,245 on February 1, 1898. That year, he also

Public domain.

entered a twelve-string harp guitar in a New York competition, where it was judged "superior" and at which the Parisian Academy of Inventors awarded him a gold medal and an honorary membership.

Just after the turn of the century, Orville partnered with five other local men in a limited business partnership, although, oddly, Orville's name is not listed as a formal member of organization. Over the next few years, his day-to-day involvement with the company dwindled, and he lived on the $2,500 he had received from selling the exclusive rights to his patent in 1904 (equivalent to about $86,000 today) and his company royalties.

Like many creative types, Orville struggled with chronic mental issues later in life. Between 1907 and 1909, he was admitted to the Kalamazoo State Hospital for psychological treatment at the request of his brother Ozro. During this time, Michigan's attorney general, John E. Bird, reportedly assigned a man named William R. Fox to serve as Orville's guardian and to manage his affairs.

Moving back to New York in 1911, Orville was under the care of Dr. Madill with stints in and out of the St. Lawrence State Hospital in Ogdensburg. It was here where he died of chronic endocarditis on August 19, 1918, at the age of sixty-two. He was buried in Morningside Cemetery in Malone, New York, in his brother Lovell's family plot.

For more than eighty years, Kalamazoo was recognized as the "Home of Guitars," and at one point, 85 percent of all fretted stringed instruments manufactured in America were built here. The list of artists who play Gibson-made guitars—like the Les Paul and Flying V models—spans decades and includes Eric Clapton, Sheryl Crow, Bob Dylan, Ace Frehley, Billy Gibbons, Jimi Hendrix, B.B. King, Bob Marley, Paul McCartney, Jimmy Page, Les Paul, Elvis Presley, Keith Richards, Carlos Santana, Slash and countless others.

Gibson Guitars moved offices and operations to Nashville in 1984, but the musical legacy lives on at Heritage Guitar Inc. (HeritageGuitars.com), which was founded in 1985 in the factory at 225 Parsons Street, a site added to the National Register of Historic Places in 2022.

ALBERT J. WHITE

An early life of turmoil, hard work and self-motivation was the foundation on which one of Kalamazoo's eminent contractors built his business and reputation.

In 2021, a detailed history of the White family was published by Washington County historian Jeremy Elliott. The piece notes that a formerly enslaved woman had gained freedom for herself and her nine children in the mid- to late 1820s, walking from Perquimans County, North Carolina, to Washington County, Indiana. Among her children was a boy named Dennison, who, years later, met and married Emmaline Newby. This couple had four children, the second being Albert J. White, born in Canton, Indiana, on February 6, 1861.

When Albert was just a toddler, tragedy struck the White family. Confederate general John Hunt Morgan and his "Morgan Raiders"—a band of 1,800 Confederate cavalrymen—ventured into Indiana and Ohio in the summer of 1863, causing havoc for the local communities. Although no documentation exists, as many of the victims of these attacks were Black, it is believed that Dennison was killed as he tried to stop the marauders.

The 1870 census showed Emmaline and her children living in Howard County, Indiana; although, shortly thereafter, Albert was removed from third grade and sent to live as a hired hand for a local farmer. For eight years, the boy worked the fields, and by age seventeen, he'd made his way to Richland, Michigan, to work for farmer Samuel Brown. It was here that Albert met a local brick and stone mason. He spent his summers on the farm and his winters apprenticing, for free, for the mason. He became a journeyman at the age of twenty-three, and two years later, in 1886, he opened his own construction firm.

Courtesy of Annette Taborn.

The next summer, Albert wed Fannie Blanche Phillips of Oshtemo Township. They went on to have three children, amass considerable property throughout the area and become pillars of the community. Albert served thirty years as a deacon for the Second Baptist Church, while Fannie was active with the Women's Temperance Movement, Needlework Guild and Civic Improvement League and was vice-president of the National Colored Baptist Women's Convention.

Over the course of forty years, Albert and his crew of fifty men—both Black and white—helped construct some of the region's most noted buildings. Top of the list was Western State Normal School's first building at the top of Prospect Hill, known first as Heritage Hall and later as East Hall, dedicated on November 23, 1905. Designed by architect Ernest W. Arnold, the stately three-story brick building was flanked by six Greek pillars and topped with a cupola. Central to the college's activities until the campus moved west in the 1940s, the building was later used as the university's archive center. In 1978, it was added to the National Register of Historic Places, and in 1990, the entire East Campus was added as the "Western State Normal School Historic District." Both sites were delisted on March 7, 2017, after modern additions impacted their historical integrity. Today, the expanded building is home to the WMU Alumni Center, and in 2024, a permanent wall display honoring Albert's contributions to the building's early history was unveiled on the first floor of Heritage Hall.

Other projects in Albert's masonry portfolio include the Kalamazoo Vegetable Parchment paper mill (among other mills), the first addition to Borgess Hospital, the Temple B'nai Israel Synagogue (since razed), the third Kalamazoo Central High School and additions to both original 1873 Plainwell High School and former Nazareth College in Kalamazoo.

The physical strains of four decades of hard labor caught up with Albert, and he retired in 1926. Four years later, on February 26, 1930, he was hospitalized with a degenerative spinal condition, which led to avascular necrosis, a loss of blood supply to the bones resulting in tissue death and an excruciating infection. He passed away on May 16, 1930, and was buried alongside Fannie (who died on August 15, 1943) in Kalamazoo's Riverside Cemetery.

WILLIAM SHAKESPEARE JR.

The acclaimed writer William Shakespeare had no known ties to the world of fishing, but the William Shakespeare Jr.—who called Kalamazoo his hometown—had one thing in common with the English bard. He was a master of his craft.

As the son of Michigan's youngest enlisted man in the Civil War (at the age of seventeen), William had big shoes to fill. Born in 1869 to Lydia A. (Markley) and William Shakespeare Sr., young William watched his father march through life as a businessman, banker, lawyer, community leader and editor/proprietor of the *Kalamazoo Gazette.*

Near the turn of the century, William Jr. honed his love of fishing into a recreational legacy. In 1896, he patented the level-winding fishing reel, which allowed anglers to wind their line back onto the spool evenly without having to guide it with their thumb. It was said to be a superior design concept, unlike anything else on the market at the time, and one that shaped the future of fishing equipment.

The next year, he founded The William Shakespeare Jr. Company (later renamed to The Shakespeare Company). By the time it was incorporated in 1905, he had employed about a dozen people who assembled a growing line of gear inside his factory on Water Street. During the early 1900s, William continued to develop equipment and other items specifically for fisherman, including a line guide for a fishing rod (1910) and a fishing reel (1911).

William moved his thriving operations to a large factory building at 419 North Pitcher Street in downtown Kalamazoo in 1913. A one-story Art Deco–style office building—emblazoned with the name "SHAKESPEARE"—was later added just to the west of the factory.

As World War I (and later, World War II) took priority, Shakespeare Products was established to assist in the efforts. Production lines were

Kalamazoo Public Library.

converted to manufacture motor fuses, automobile carburetors and controls for aircraft, jeeps and tanks. Despite the global turmoil, Shakespeare's fishing gear was being sold by more than five thousand dealers around the country, making the company a leader in its field.

Throughout the 1930s and 1940s, William continued to invent and distribute new lines of gear, lures and other fishing equipment. In 1939, he invented a "Backlash" Brake, which prevented spools from backlashing. In the mid-1940s, he introduced the President Reel followed by the Wonderod®, which was invented by a famous chemical engineer named Dr. Arthur M. Howland, ultimately revolutionizing the fishing rod market and making bamboo and steel virtually obsolete in rod construction. He also developed a two-gear direct-drive reel and was one of the first to manufacture monofilament line from raw materials.

By the time Shakespeare's hit its fiftieth anniversary in 1947, William's son, Henry, was at the helm. By then, rod production had moved to South Carolina, incorporated as the Columbia Products Company, followed by the relocation of the company headquarters. For a brief period, the Flexible Controls Division remained in Kalamazoo. In the late 1970s, The Shakespeare Company became a subsidiary of California-based Anthony Industries Inc., and today, it is a subsidiary of South Carolina–based Pure Fishing, a global leader in tackle.

Outside of the fishing world, William held other mechanical patents and once served as a traveling salesman of patent medicines. In 1918, Kalamazoo instated a commission-manager form of government—one of the first cities in the United States to do so—and William was one of nine men to serve. He was later appointed as vice-mayor (1923–24) and mayor (1933–34), ending his service with back-to-back terms from 1938 to 1940.

William was married three times and had four children. He died on June 25, 1950, at the age of eighty, and was buried in Kalamazoo's Riverside Cemetery.

The distinctive Art Deco–style building that once served as the Shakespeare offices remains a vital part of the downtown community, serving as Shakespeare's Pub (ShakespearesPub.com) since July 19, 2003.

GEORGE D. TAYLOR

Celery is one of the most common vegetables in America today, but in the mid-nineteenth century, it was considered a rare delicacy. Reserved for the rich, it was served in tall crystal vases filled with ice water to keep the stalks crunchy. It is widely believed that the first place in which celery was commercially grown in the United States (for consumers, markets and restaurants) was Kalamazoo, Michigan.

In the fall of 1855, a fifty-three-year-old horticulturalist and nurseryman from Scotland named George Taylor immigrated to Kalamazoo with his second wife, a very pregnant Jane (Dodds), and their three children, Isabella, Andrew and James. George's younger brothers, James and Andrew, had already taken up residency in the area. Much of George's autobiographical history is chronicled on Michigan Genealogy on the Web (part of the USGenWeb Project) at migenweb.org (the following quotes are from this source).

"Brother James…proposed to let me have a piece of his land opposite the Mountain Home Cemetery, as a nursery. And so I looked out to find a house for my family most convenient to this. The only one I could find was an old one at the corner below the cemetery belonging to Charles Stuart, and the rent he charged was 2 dollars a week. I thought this very high for such a house, but was assured that I could not rent a house any cheaper."

George spent that fall and winter working as a farmhand, chopping wood and cutting ice. The following spring, he had his land ploughed and, over the years, planted evergreens (specifically Norway spruce), ornamental plants, roses, flowers, fruit trees and vegetables, including cabbage, tomatoes, green peas, sweet corn and celery. He sold produce at his brother's meat market and to an Englishman named Cox, who ran a small grocery store on Burdick Street. In time, he introduced celery to local hotels and restaurants.

Public domain.

"The next year Mr. Acre of the Burdick House wanted me to bring him a dozen or two every week, then of course the Kalamazoo House had to be supplied in the same way, then certain private families wanted a couple of heads. Before long the thing went on like a house afire, almost everybody wanted it. For nearly ten years I was the principal grower of celery and I made well out by it, as the price at the hotels was never below 50 cent a dozen."

In September 1860, George's wife, Jane, died of consumption. Two years later, he visited Scotland and returned to Kalamazoo with a cousin, Jane (Willence or Whillence), whom he married on January 1, 1863. Sadness would strike the family twice in the coming months. In August 1863, George's nineteen-year-old son, Andrew, drowned in a nearby lake while duck hunting. Then shortly after that, Jane died while giving birth to the couple's son.

The years that followed were busy for George and his nursery business. In 1866, he purchased twenty acres from Sabin Nichols on Grand Prairie for $1,500 but sold it a year later "at a pretty fair price." He then acquired twenty acres on Portage Street near Reed Street, where he ultimately built a house and operated the Portage Nursery with his son James.

George married his fourth wife, Susan (Carter), in 1870 and retired in 1881, selling the nursery to his son James. Susan died in 1889, and George himself passed away on August 21, 1891, at the age of eighty-eight. He and many members of his family were buried in Mountain Home Cemetery on West Main Street.

A historical marker recognizing George and his contributions to making Kalamazoo a "Celery City" was erected at the intersection of Crosstown Parkway and Park Street in 1959. Farther south, the city of Portage is the home of Celery Flats Interpretive Area, featuring exhibits about this early agricultural industry.

ALBERT MAY TODD

Essential oils have become all the rage in recent years, with various scents being widely promoted for health and healing. More than a century and a half ago, one curious, zealous and innovative man dedicated his life to mentha (mint), earning himself the moniker "Peppermint King of Kalamazoo."

Alfred and Mary Ann (Hovey) Todd moved from Upstate New York to St. Joseph County, Michigan, in the late 1830s with five of their eventually ten children, settling near Nottawa. Their youngest child, Albert May, was born on June 3, 1850.

After graduating from Sturgis High School, nineteen-year-old Albert borrowed $100, leased five acres from his father to grow mint and founded the A.M. Todd Company with his brother Oliver. Four years later, Albert set off to study chemistry at Northwestern University in Evanston, Illinois, but due to some sort of illness, he left and traipsed through Europe to recuperate. There, he continued his interest in mint and brought several cultivars back to the United States.

Albert later returned to college, earning a master's degree in chemistry from the University of Michigan. He also bought out his brother's company shares and expanded operations, amassing over ten thousand acres where he grew, harvested and processed mint, along with undertaking other agricultural enterprises, like raising shorthorn cattle, growing onions and potatoes and producing hemp for rope during World War I. During his career, Albert operated three farm towns, including Campania near Fennville, Mentha in Van Buren County's Pine Grove Township and Sylvia Range.

In 1875, Albert patented his Crystal White double-distilled peppermint, which won awards at the U.S. Centennial Exposition in Philadelphia in 1876; the Chicago World's Fair Exposition in 1893; the Paris World's Fair

Kalamazoo Public Library.

Exposition in 1900; the Pan American World's Fair Exposition in Buffalo, New York, in 1901; and the St. Louis World's Fair Exposition in 1904.

By the turn of the century, the A.M. Todd Company was the largest mint producer on the planet, growing 90 percent of the world's mint near Kalamazoo and supplying well-known companies like Wrigley in Chicago. The original Todd factory operated on the southwest corner of Rose Street and Kalamazoo Avenue until 1929, when a new facility opened north of downtown on Douglas Avenue. The family owned the company until 2011, when it was acquired by Swiss flavoring giant Wild Flavors (which, in turn, was sold to Chicago-based Archer Daniels Midland in 2014 for $3 billion).

Beyond minting, Albert dabbled in politics. He unsuccessfully ran for Michigan governor under the Prohibition Party in 1894, coming in fourth place. He did serve one term in the U.S. House of Representatives (March 4, 1897, to March 8, 1899), representing Michigan's Third District.

He was also a noted bibliophile, owning over eleven thousand volumes, including illuminated manuscripts and clay tablets dating to the twenty-third century BCE, as well as more than two hundred paintings, sculptures, pottery and porcelain pieces from around the world. His contributions to the Kalamazoo School Board led to the creation of the Kalamazoo Public Museum. Collections can also be found at Western Michigan University, University of Michigan and in the A.M. Todd Rare Book Room at the Upjohn Library of Kalamazoo College.

Albert died in Kalamazoo in 1931 at the age of eighty-one and was buried in Mountain Home Cemetery along with his wife, Augusta Margarette (Allman), and several of their children.

After the onset of World War II, the Todd Farm at Campania became a wildlife refuge and was sold to the State of Michigan in 1950. It is now part of the Allegan State Game Area and is headquarters for Michigan's Department of Natural Resources' Farm Unit.

In 1965, a five-story dilapidated nineteenth-century barn in Campania was purchased from the state and transported in pieces to the Gilmore Car Museum in Hickory Corners (see pages 100–101) to house a collection of vintage vehicles. The Michigan Barn Preservation Network honored it as its "Michigan Barn of the Year" in 2004.

JACOB KINDLEBERGER

Despite being dealt a losing hand at birth, a determined immigrant with a head for business and a heart of gold stepped out from his father's shadow and advanced the industry in which they both worked.

Born on February 28, 1875, in Alsace-Lorraine, Germany, to Johannes "John" and Otilda (Fraelich) Kindleberger, Jacob L. Kindleberger immigrated with his family to the United States when he was just five years old.

John, who had worked in the paper industry in Europe, found meager employment in Ohio. Young Jacob was uneducated and visually impaired but was still forced to take odd jobs to help support his family. At the age of ten, he earned just a quarter a day working in the rag room at the mill where his father was employed. Three years later, Jacob was a machine operator making thirty cents an hour, but life for the Kindlebergers remained bleak.

When Jacob was fifteen, he and some other teenagers crashed a church meeting, and that action changed his life—for the better. Inspired by the words of the preacher, Jacob finally saw a path to a positive future. He eventually had his eyes examined and was fitted with glasses. Then he began attending school to learn how to read and write. He even considered dedicating his life to the ministry.

At the age of twenty-one, Jacob left the paper mill and became a school janitor in order to attend night classes. From there, he enrolled in the Academy at Wesleyan College at Delaware, working as a salesman to pay tuition. In the fall of 1901, he advanced to the college program but quit in his third year due to excessive eye strain.

Having found financial success selling steam cookers and making up to $100 a week, Jacob continued to work toward a better life than the one his father had. Yet in an apparent step backward, he took a position as a paper salesman (making just $15 a week), recognizing the opportunities such a profession might bring. For the next thirteen years, Jacob mastered his territory—the entire United States, Mexico and Canada—and built an extensive network that would serve him throughout his career.

On December 7, 1905, Jacob married Lucinda Drusilla (Faulkner), and their only child, Joseph Burns, was born in West Carrollton, Ohio, in 1906.

Parchment Community Library.

Three years later, Jacob visited Kalamazoo at the request of his brother-in-law Harry Zimmerman. The two discussed the need for a parchment paper factory in town, and Jacob was soon securing funding to bring that idea into fruition. With $50,000 in capital, Jacob founded the Kalamazoo Vegetable Parchment Company (KVP) along the banks of the Kalamazoo River on October 27, 1909. His family then moved to Kalamazoo, living at first with the Zimmermans, then taking up residency in the former Kalamazoo Sugar Beet factory office building and later building a house at 521 Riverview Drive.

Jacob envisioned a "model community for the world," creating a positive environment—both on and off the job—for his staff to thrive. KVP had among the highest wages within the local paper industry, and the company even purchased nearby land and resold it to the employees to give them affordable opportunities to build their own homes.

On July 28, 1930, the Kindlebergers donated thirty-eight acres to what became the Village of Parchment for a community park. Valued at about $35,000, Kindelberger Park was dedicated on Saturday, June 17, 1933, with sports courts and fields, miles of walking trails and a large formal garden. Picnic tables, pavilions, a gazebo, playgrounds and an outdoor stage were added later. Although Parchment no longer produces paper, the community is proud of its heritage as the "Paper City" and Kindelberger Park, which received a Michigan Historical Marker in 2019 and remains the "Jewel of Parchment."

Jacob died on January 1, 1947, at the age of seventy-one. He was buried in Riverside Cemetery alongside his wife and son.

MORRIS MARKIN

One of the premier TV sitcoms of the late 1970s and early 1980s was *Taxi*, based on the fictional Sunshine Cab Company of Manhattan, New York. During the show's five seasons (and 114 episodes), its ensemble cast was nominated for thirty-one Emmy Awards—winning eighteen—including Outstanding Comedy Series three years in a row. The classic yellow cabs featured were manufactured in downtown Kalamazoo by the king of the taxi industry.

Morris Markin was born on July 15, 1893, as Solomon (Zalman) Tamarkin to a Jewish family in Smolensk, Russia. He immigrated to the United States at the age of nineteen with just $1.65 in his pocket, leaving Antwerp, Belgium, aboard the *Kroonland* and arriving at Ellis Island on November 26, 1912.

He was broke and spoke no English, but a kindhearted janitor loaned him twenty-five dollars, and he was soon on his way to Chicago to live with his uncle. There, he went right to work, earning a living and making enough money to bring his siblings to America. For a brief time, the young man worked in the clothing industry and made a fortune supplying uniforms to the U.S. Army during World War I.

By 1919, Morris was making inroads into the automotive industry and running a taxi fleet. At the time, there were two primary companies operating in Chicago: Yellow Cab (founded in 1910 by John Hertz, the founder of today's Hertz Car Rentals) and Checker Taxi (owned by George Hilsky).

Commonwealth Motors in Joliet, Illinois, was manufacturing cabs for Hilsky, using their own chassis with bodies from Lomberg Auto Manufacturing Co. After Abe Lomberg failed to repay a $15,000 business loan to Morris in October 1921, he was forced to sign over the company, and

Public domain.

it was merged with Markin Automobile Body to form the Checker Cab Manufacturing Co. With that, Morris was not only running the cabs, but he was also making them.

Morris soon acquired the Yellow Cab Company from Hertz (including one-third of the company that had been sold to Parmalee Transportation Company), making him the king of the Midwest cab industry. That title didn't come without its share of problems, like the firebombing of the Morris's Chicago home. He soon set his sights on a smaller, more welcoming town and acquired two vacant factories on the north side of downtown Kalamazoo. The former Handley-Knight plant on North Pitcher Street was purchased in May 1923, followed by the purchase of the Dort Motor Car Company building on South Pitcher Street.

For decades, Checker Cabs rolled off the Kalamazoo assembly lines as Morris expanded operations again and again to meet demand. By 1965, over a quarter of the cabs on the streets in the country were built in Kalamazoo. In the 1960s, Morris also ventured into the consumer car market, releasing the A10 Superba sedan and station wagons, later renamed the A12 Marathon, as well as a limousine model (which was used by the U.S. State Department for overseas diplomat transport) and a unique stretch version of the station wagon called the Aerobus (available in both six- and eight-door options).

On July 12, 1999, the final Checker Cab rolled off the Kalamazoo assembly line. That same month, the last Checker cab in New York City (named "Janie" by owner Earl Johnson) was retired from service, with nearly one million miles on its odometer, driven by Johnson starting in 1978.

Morris died in Kalamazoo on July 8, 1970 (at the age of seventy-six), and was buried in the Mount Carmel Cemetery in Glendale, New York, alongside his wife, Bessie, and their four children.

The 160-acre Markin Estate on North Westnedge Avenue in Cooper Township was purchased by the City of Kalamazoo in 1970 and turned into Maple Glen Park. The following year, the Kalamazoo Garden Club began utilizing the home for its offices and programs. Ownership of the estate was transferred to Kalamazoo County in 1985, and in 1997, it was renamed Markin Glen Park (featuring a thirty-eight-site campground, hiking trails, a swimming beach and tennis courts).

SUZANNE UPJOHN (DELANO) PARISH

Suzanne Upjohn DeLano was a descendant of two noted Kalamazoo families—her mother, Dorothy, was the daughter William E. and Rachel (Babcock) Upjohn, and her father, Herman Allen, was the grandson of William Smith DeLano—whose historic farm is owned and operated by the Kalamazoo Nature Center as the DeLano Homestead. Here maternal aunt Genevieve (Upjohn) Gilmore was the wife of noted businessman Donald S. Gilmore (see pages 100–101).

Born on November 13, 1922, in New York City, Sue spent her early years in France before settling in Kalamazoo in 1929. As a child, Sue had a passion for horses and dreamed of becoming a veterinarian, but a serious fall in 1942 led to a change in her hobbies. With her mother's encouragement, she signed up for flying lessons, and within a year, she had earned her private pilot certificate and commercial pilot certificate. By the time she was twenty-one, she had clocked over 350 hours in the air.

With World War II underway, Sue joined the newly formed Women Airforce Service Pilots (WASP) in 1944. According to the U.S. Army, "in the 16 months WASP existed, more than 25,000 women applied for training; only 1,879 candidates were accepted. Among them, 1,074 successfully completed the grueling program."

WASP graduates were assigned to more than one hundred air bases nationwide, serving as test pilots and freeing male pilots for combat. They also ferried aircraft to and from air bases and towed targets for aerial antiaircraft gunnery training—a high-risk operation. Sue was in the 44-W-G class stationed at Bryan Army Air Base in Texas, where she flew AT-6 and BT-13 planes until the program was disbanded on December 20, 1944.

Courtesy of Air Zoo.

Back home, Sue longed for a career in aviation, something unheard of for women at the time. After repeated rejections, including one from her uncle Donald Gilmore to work as a private pilot for The Upjohn Company, Sue volunteered as a driver for the Red Cross Motor Corps, transferring soldiers from Fort Custer in Battle Creek to a rehabilitation center set up at the W.K. Kellogg Manor House on nearby Gull Lake.

In 1948, Sue married Chicago-born World War II marine veteran Preston "Pete" Parish, and they went on to have five children (two daughters and three sons).

Like Sue, Pete had a love for planes and flying. In the late 1950s, he purchased a share in a single-engine 35C Bonanza followed by a Stearman, an AT-6, a Grumman Wildcat and a P-40 Warhawk. The couple founded the Kalamazoo Aviation History Museum in 1977 to showcase their collection. An expanded 200,000-square-foot Air Zoo opened in 2011. Featured displays include Sue's dessert pink Warhawk, a plane she flew in countless air shows for more than twenty-five years until October 1993, as well as her signature pink flight suit and WASP uniform.

By the time she retired from flying in March 1999, at the age of seventy-six, Sue had accumulated more seven thousand flying hours. She was the first woman inducted into the Experimental Aircraft Association Warbird Hall of Fame. She was also inducted into the WMU College of Aviation Hall of Fame, Michigan Aviation Hall of Fame, Warbird Hall of Fame and Michigan Military and Veterans Hall of Honor. In 1984, she received a WASP World War II Victory Medal, and on March 10, 2010, she was presented a Congressional Gold Medal by President Barack Obama. She was active with the Michigan Space Center in Jackson, Warbirds of America, Flying Tigers Association and P-40 Warhawk Pilots Association.

Sue was also an actor at the Kalamazoo Civic Theatre, and in August 1998, the 260-seat Suzanne D. Parish Theatre was dedicated. The Suzanne Upjohn DeLano Parish Foundation has awarded funding to worthy organizations, such as the Kalamazoo Civic Theatre, Kalamazoo Gospel Mission and Kalamazoo Nature Center.

Sue died on May 12, 2010, at the age of eighty-seven at Smoke Tree Ranch in Palm Springs, California, where she spent her winters.

MELVIN RICHARD HARDING

A country boy from the Bluegrass State made his way to Southern Michigan, where he built a retail empire that remains active today, with a handful of descendants still working for the company that bears the family name.

Born on January 5, 1906, in Hickman, Kentucky (the county seat of Fulton County), Melvin Richard "Mel" Harding was the tenth of twelve children of Horace and Leila (Blakemore) Harding. Around the time of his birth, the population of Hickman was around 1,600—it would peak in the 1970s at just over 3,000.

Little is known about Mel's childhood. Descendants say he never made it to high school and worked with his father, taking fruits and vegetables grown on the family farm to neighbors and the nearby market by mule-drawn wagon. These early community activities would foreshadow Mel's later life, leaving a legacy that remains today.

In the 1920s, Mel and his brother Horace were hired by Kroger, a grocery company founded in 1883 in Cincinnati, Ohio. It was through this job that the brothers made their way to Michigan. In Michigan, Mel met Ruth Elizabeth Schultz; they were married on December 18, 1933, and went on to have two sons, Tom and Larry, and one daughter, Judy.

After years with Kroger, Mel took the initiative to open his own store at 126 North Riverview Drive in Parchment in 1944 (razed in 2019). It was a small operation, taking up just 7,500 square feet, and Mel proudly called it Harding's Friendly Market. A second store was opened in the former Slager and Bos Grocery at 812 South Westnedge Avenue, followed by an acquisition of Bob's Market at Portage and Cork Streets, both in 1946.

Mel was on a roll, and he was just getting started.

Courtesy of the Harding family.

The February 15, 1950 edition of the *Kalamazoo Gazette* noted the development of a new shopping center on Monroe Street in Allegan. Mel spent between $20,000 and $25,000 to construct a one-hundred-by-fifty-foot store along the Kalamazoo River. The article referenced that Mel also owned markets in Kalamazoo, Plainwell, Schoolcraft, Paw Paw and Vicksburg by that time.

Over the years, Mel added to his grocery empire. One noteworthy project was his store in the Southland Mall on the corner of Milham Road and South Westnedge Avenue, which opened in the summer of 1960. Comprising 160,000 square feet, the entire shopping complex was three times larger than any other in town at the time, with room for more than a dozen stores. Mel opened his largest Harding's to date at the end of that complex, with a Kroger just a stone's throw away to the south. Somehow, Mel knew the area would develop over time, and about twenty-two years later, Crossroads Mall opened in the neighborhood.

"My dad was a great businessman," recalled Mel's daughter, Judy Berger. "I was always amazed about his visions and knowing where a good store would work."

Throughout his career, Mel opened about forty Harding's locations in Southern Michigan and Northern Indiana, many of them still in operation today and a handful run by the entrepreneur's descendants.

Mel was also active in various organizations and was elected to the board of the Grand Rapids Wholesale Grocery Company (which later became Spartan Stores, ultimately merging with Nash Finch Company in 2013 to become SpartanNash), serving alongside notables like Fred Meijer, Roman Feldpausch and L.V. Eberhard. In 1961, he was president of the board for Spartan. He was also a director with the Muller-Grocers Baking Company of Grand Rapids.

With a philosophy that "Our customers deserve the best in quality produce and the friendliest service we can provide," Harding's Friendly Markets remain vital to many area communities. Mel's son Tom went into the family business, as did Tom's son Tim, who owns eight of the twenty-eight stores still in operation in Michigan.

Melvin Harding died on March 23, 1985, and was buried in Mount Ever-Rest Memorial Park in Kalamazoo, alongside Ruth.

LARRY JAMES BELL

A commitment to the environment, the arts and craft beer have led to a unique legacy for this brewer turned philanthropist.

Larry James Bell was born on June 9, 1958, the youngest of three sons of Rollin and Lorraine (Michaels) Bell. Growing up in Park Forest, Illinois (a southern suburb of Chicago), he was a Cubs fan and a Boy Scout with dreams of becoming a jazz drummer. At Rich Central High School in Olympia Fields, Illinois, Larry was on the tennis team for two years, played percussion in the band, began collecting beer cans, joined the Sierra Club and worked on the school newspaper, serving as editor-in-chief during his senior year.

After graduating in 1976, Larry enrolled at Kalamazoo College, where he studied political science, history and music, working at the newly opened Sarkozy Bakery. It was there that a coworker introduced him to homebrewing, something that changed the trajectory of his life. He started brewing beer in the basement of his house, which led to the opening of a homebrew shop in July 1983. Just two years later, with a handful of investors, Larry founded Kalamazoo Brewing Company, selling his first beer on September 19, 1985.

Those early days were tough, but Larry forged ahead, pushing the boundaries within the slowly evolving brewing community. Oberon, launched in 1992 as SolSun, became one of two flagship beers known around the country. The other, Two Hearted IPA, hit the market in 1997 and is regarded as the best in its category in America.

June 11, 1993, was a milestone day for Larry. After working with the Michigan legislature to change state laws to allow breweries to sell draft beer in their own taprooms, his Eccentric Café at 355 East Kalamazoo

Courtesy of Larry J. Bell.

Avenue became the first brewery taproom in the state to sell its own beer by the glass on premise.

Larry continued to grow his operations in Kalamazoo and beyond. In 1996, he added a beer garden to the north side of the Eccentric Café, and in 2001, he purchased five acres in nearby Comstock for a new production facility, rebranding as Bell's Brewery. By 2013, Larry had bought out all his investors to acquire sole ownership in the company, and a love of the Upper Peninsula led to him open Upper Hand Brewery in Escanaba in 2014. After thirty-eight years in the industry, Larry sold all his operations to Lion Little World Beverages of Australia in late 2021.

With more time and money on his hands, Larry set out to make a stronger community impact with the establishment of the Larry and Shannon Bell Charitable Fund. Donations have since been made to the Irving S. Gilmore International Piano Festival, Kalamazoo College, Boys and Girls Club of Kalamazoo, Michigan State University Hospitality School, Wellspring–Cory Terry & Dancers, Gulliver Historical Society and Three Lakes Academy in Curtis, Michigan.

After surviving cancer in July 2020, Larry also made contributions to the National Kidney Foundation of Michigan, Bronson Hospital Foundation and North Country Trail (NCT), America's longest scenic route. He recently set out on a personal quest to hike the entire 1,180-mile Michigan section of the NCT, in short day trip treks, something he hopes to accomplish by 2026.

Another philanthropic endeavor under development is The Larry J. Bell Library Foundation, which will include a private research facility as well as a public display of Larry's vast collections, including maps, brewery memorabilia, prints, ceramics and more.

Among his accolades, Larry received the Brewers Association Recognition Award in 2010, the Michigan Brewers Guild's Tom Burns Award in 2012 and The Sierra Club Michigan Chapter Environmentalist of the Year in 2022. Kalamazoo College presented him with its Distinguished Achievement Award in 2010, and on June 12, 2023, Larry was presented an honorary degree in humane letters and was also the college's commencement speaker.

EDUCATORS, SOLDIERS AND POLITICIANS

ABRAHAM LINCOLN

To date, only one president in U.S. history has hailed from Michigan (Gerald R. Ford was raised in Grand Rapids), but over the years, a dozen men who were or would later become president passed through Michigan—Kalamazoo, specifically.

In his lifetime, Abraham Lincoln made just one known trip to Michigan, four years before he was elected as America's sixteenth president. It was believed to be the only time in a nearly two-year period that he left Illinois.

On Wednesday, August 27, 1856, the clean-shaven, six-foot-four, forty-seven-year-old lawyer and former congressman from Illinois made his way by train from Chicago to downtown Kalamazoo (population: ten thousand) for a Republican rally in support of presidential candidate James C. Fremont. Earlier that summer, during the Republican National Convention in Philadelphia, Lincoln had placed second as the party's vice presidential pick, ultimately losing to William Lewis Dayton (64.73 percent to 13.61 percent).

Hezekiah G. Wells of the Republican executive committee had written a letter on July 24, 1856, inviting Lincoln to speak at the Kalamazoo rally. Lincoln's reply, dated August 4, stated, in part, "It would afford me great pleasure to be with you, and I will do so if possible; but I cannot promise positively." This original letter, written on congressional stationery, is kept in the archives at the Kalamazoo Valley Museum. Lincoln sent a follow-up letter on August 21, noting, "At last I am able to say, no accident preventing, I will be with you on the 27th."

Rally day found the main streets of downtown Kalamazoo adorned with banners as bands performed and people from around the state began gathering around the four stages set up in Bronson Park. According to the *Niles Enquirer*, attendance was estimated to be over thirty thousand.

Author's collection.

It is said that Lincoln's train pulled into the station late and he had to rush five blocks from the depot to the park in order to take the stage at 2:00 p.m., where he delivered a 2,781-word speech primarily addressing concerns about the expansion of slavery in about sixteen and a half minutes.

While the *Kalamazoo Gazette* covered the rally, it was a reporter from the *Detroit Daily Advertiser* who diligently hand recorded Lincoln's speech, which was published two days later, along with a recap of the day's events. A transcript of the speech can be found on the Kalamazoo Public Library website, KPL.gov.

The exact location where Lincoln stood during his speech remains unknown, but in 1957, the State of Michigan erected a historical marker in the southwest corner of the park denoting the date of the speech (it had been approved the year prior). It is also a mystery where Lincoln spent the night before returning to Chicago the day after the rally, although it may have been the Burdick Hotel (today known as the Radisson Plaza Hotel).

During his brief stay, Lincoln did make time to network with at least a couple locals. In a letter dated August 31, 1860, sent to the Honorable Zachariah Chandler (one of the other rally speakers), Lincoln wrote, "I very well remember meeting you at Kalamazoo in 1856. I very well remember the jovial elderly lady, and wife of an M.C. with whom we took tea, calling you 'Zach Chander.'"

Even more than a century and a half later, Lincoln's visit to Kalamazoo remains a proud moment in time. In the fall of 2012, the Kalamazoo Abraham Lincoln Project, now known as the Kalamazoo Abraham Lincoln Institute (KalamazooLincolnInstitute.org), was formed to further the cultural and educational elements of this historic occasion. On August 27, 2023, 167 years to the day after Lincoln's Kalamazoo visit, a privately funded seven-foot bronze statue of Lincoln was unveiled in Bronson Park. Sculpted by William Wolfe of Terre Haute, Indiana, it depicts Lincoln holding his speech close to his heart, his other hand signaling to the crowd.

DWIGHT BRYANT WALDO

One of Michigan's top collegiate leaders had a fascination with President Abraham Lincoln and, for years, kept an interesting pet—a parrot named Jimmy Boy.

Dwight Bryant Waldo was born on June 13, 1864, in Arcade, New York, to Simeon Smith and Martha Ann (Bryant) Waldo. The family relocated to Michigan around 1873, settling in Plainwell, where his father was a grocer and where Dwight graduated high school in 1879.

In 1881, Dwight made his way to Michigan Agricultural College (Michigan State University) to begin his collegiate career—one that spanned fifty-five years from student to teacher and, eventually, principal or president. He earned a master's degree from Albion College, where he was a member of Sigma Chi and later taught history and German in the preparatory department. Between 1889 and 1891, he took graduate-level courses at Harvard University but did not earn a degree.

On New Year's Eve 1890, Dwight married Minnie (Strong) in St. Joseph County, Michigan. The couple was soon off to Wisconsin, where Dwight taught history and political economics at Beloit College for two years. He was back at Albion College by 1892, serving as the chair of political science and economics. The first three Waldo children were born in the late twentieth century—Rollin Dwight (1891–92), Hubert Strong (1893) and Ruth Genevieve (1896)—not long before the family made their way to Michigan's Upper Peninsula.

The Northern State Teachers' College was opened in 1899 in Marquette, and Dwight was named its first principal, serving in this position for five years. During his tenure, he supervised the construction of the Peter White Hall of Science, dedicated in 1902, and Longyear Hall, which was completed in 1907. Years later, the 160-acre Longyear Forest was established on the campus, with Waldo Pond being named for the university's first principal.

Dwight B. Waldo and his pet parrot, Jimmy Boy. *Zhang Collection, Western Michigan University Archives.*

After Minnie died of cancer in January 1903, she was buried in her hometown of Vicksburg, Michigan. The next year, on September 14, Dwight married a former student, Eliza Lilian (Trudgeon), and three more daughters would grace the family over the subsequent years—Elizabeth (1908), Barbara (1911) and Dorothy (1919).

On April 1, 1904, Dwight was elected president of the new Western State Normal College, which had opened in Kalamazoo. In the beginning, it was a two-year institution, but it evolved into a four-year teachers' college under Dwight's guidance. In addition to running the school, Dwight was also one of the first instructors and quickly became recognized as one of the top academic leaders in the country. By the early 1920s, his annual salary was reported at about $6,000 (about $100,000 today).

Two decades into his service at Western State, Dwight accepted the position of interim president of the Bellingham State Normal School in Washington State. He started in April 1922 and served just fifteen months while leading a full-scale review of the school's program and helping them search for his successor. By July 1923, he had returned to his desk at Western State, where he stayed until he retired in 1936.

Throughout his career, Dwight was presented honorary degrees from Kalamazoo College and Michigan Agricultural College, served as president of the National Normal School Presidents, was one of the founders and a former president of the American Association of Teachers' Colleges, was president of the State Political Science Association, led the normal school section of the National Education Association and was involved in the Michigan Intercollegiate Athletic Association.

Dwight died on October 28, 1939, at the age of seventy-five, and his ashes were interred in the cornerstone of Western State's Heritage Hall (see pages 36–37). Just days later, the $270,000 Waldo Stadium sports facility was dedicated in his honor. Waldo Library, where Dwight's Abraham Lincoln collection is archived, was opened on campus in 1958 (it was expanded in 1967 and renovated and expanded again in 1991). There is even a giant boulder near Oakland and Stadium Drives that bears his name.

JOSEPH BURCHNALL WESTNEDGE

Have you ever wondered how Westnedge Avenue, which stretches fifteen miles between D Avenue in Cooper Township and Osterhouse Avenue in Portage, got its name?

Joseph Burchnall Westnedge was born on August 16, 1872, to Thomas B. and Mary (Burchnall) Westnedge. His maternal grandparents, Dorothy and Joseph Burchnall, were early brewers in Kalamazoo. Joseph was the third of four children, including his sisters, Caroline and Sarah, and brother, Richard.

In January 1893, Joseph enrolled in the Preparatory Department of Kalamazoo College (K) and advanced as an unclassified freshman with no set course of study. While at K, he was a halfback on the first winning football team in 1895, and in 1898, he was a fullback and captain on the first undefeated, untied team in that college's history. Nearly a century later, Joseph was one of fourteen individuals inducted into the inaugural class of the Kalamazoo College Athletic Hall of Fame, and a plaque honoring them hangs in the lobby of the Anderson Athletic Center.

Joseph's military career began when he enlisted as a private in the Michigan Light Guard (later known as the Michigan National Guard) on February 12, 1894. Over the next four years, he moved up the ranks to first lieutenant, Company C, Second Infantry. His studies were delayed when Michigan's Thirty-Second Volunteer Infantry left to fight in the Spanish American War in the spring of 1898. By this point, he had been promoted to captain. The unit remained down south until it was mustered out on November 2 that year. Back in Kalamazoo, Joseph resumed his studies and graduated in 1899, the same year his brother, then a military doctor, died of typhoid fever while serving in the Philippines.

National Archives.

Joseph married Eva M. Sebring on September 19, 1900, and the couple would go on to have four children. Joseph's military service continued. In 1911, he helped quell the Jackson Prison Riot; in the summer of 1913, he was sent to Houghton in Michigan's Upper Peninsula to assist with the Copper Country mining strike; and in July 1916, he served alongside General John Joseph "Black Jack" Pershing, fighting against General Francisco "Pancho" Villa in the Mexican Border War.

When the United States declared war on Germany on April 6, 1917, the now-colonel Westnedge volunteered for the new American Expeditionary Force (AEF) and was one of the few officers permitted to keep their former rank. He was soon off to France, where he served with distinction in 1917 and 1918.

About the time the Armistice was signed (November 11, 1918), Joseph was evacuated from the front with a serious case of tonsillitis. He was taken to an army hospital in Nantes, France, where his condition worsened. Just eighteen days after the war ended, the forty-six-year-old "Colonel Joe" Westnedge died of septicemia, the clinical name for blood poisoning by bacteria, the body's most extreme response to an infection. He was originally laid to rest in the American Army Cemetery no. 88 in Nantes. Two years later, his body was returned home, and the city of Kalamazoo held a funeral profession in his honor before reburying him near his brother in Riverside Cemetery.

Before his death, Joseph was considered one of Kalamazoo's most decorated soldiers. An article in the October 17, 1918 *Lansing State Journal* noted "a resolution asking the city commission to rename one of the city's prominent streets [West Street] in honor of Colonel Joseph Westnedge was adopted unanimously." That commission, the first in the city's history, was led by Mayor William E. Upjohn, with William Shakespeare Jr. (see pages 38–39) also serving. A week later, the *Battle Creek Enquirer* stated that the "people of his hometown, Kalamazoo, are now talking about supporting him [Joseph Westnedge] for congress in 1920." Six months after his death, on June 5, 1919, the Joseph B. Westnedge American Legion Post 36 received its charter (and is still active in Portage).

VERNICE MERZE TATE

The rural countryside of Isabella County, Michigan, provided little opportunity for Black Americans at the turn of the twentieth century, but one ambitious young woman would not let the barriers of gender or race keep her from conquering the world.

Vernice Merze Tate was born near Blanchard, Michigan, on February 6, 1905, to Charles and Myrtle K. (Lett) Tate. She attended the one-room Rolland Township Elementary School no. 5, also known as McCabe School, located on land owned by her family. At the age of thirteen, she entered Blanchard High School, but a fire in the late summer of 1919 scattered students to a variety of buildings in the area, and with limited resources, most graduated at the end of tenth grade. Merze was the only Black student in her class, and even though she was also the youngest, she was named valedictorian.

To prepare for college, Merze attended classes for two years at Battle Creek High School, some eighty-seven miles to the south, maintaining an A average. She then applied to the Western State Teachers College (now Western Michigan University, or WMU), where President Dwight B. Waldo (see pages 58–59) not only accepted her but also gave her a scholarship and helped her find a job to help with other expenses. In 1927, after just three years, Merze became the first Black woman to receive a bachelor's degree from the college while also recording the highest academic record in the college's history at the time.

After graduation, Merze accepted a teaching position at Crispus Attucks High School, the first segregated school built for Black Americans, in Indianapolis. While there, she started a travel club for students, taking them to places like Washington, D.C., and Niagara Falls, to expose them to different cultures, scenery and histories. During her summer breaks, Merze traveled to Columbia University in New York, where she earned her master of arts degree in 1930.

Zhang Collection, Western Michigan University Archives.

The next year, Merze received an Alpha Kappa Sorority Foreign Fellowship of $1,000, which allowed her to enroll in England's Oxford University, where she studied economics and international relations, becoming the first Black American to earn a bachelor's degree there in 1935. She also studied briefly at the University of Berlin before returning to America, where she joined the faculty at Barber-Scotia College in North Carolina as a history instructor as well as the dean of women. She later worked as the chair of social science at Bennett College in North Carolina and was the dean of women and associate professor of political science at Morgan State College.

In 1941, Merze made history again by being the first Black woman to earn a doctorate from Harvard University's Radcliffe College in Cambridge, Massachusetts. She then became the first Black woman to join the faculty of the History Department at Howard University in Washington, D.C., where she remained until her retirement in 1977.

During her lifetime, Merze mastered five languages, was awarded multiple Fulbright Scholarships, was nominated as a UNESCO representative and circled the globe twice. She was a regular visitor to the White House and met with world leaders in the Soviet Union, India, Cambodia, Australia, New Zealand and eleven African countries during the Cold War era. She authored seven books, thirty-four journal articles and forty-five review essays, working as a correspondent for a Black publication. She even attended the 1932 Olympics in Los Angeles.

Among her many awards were the Isabella County's Most Distinguished Citizen Award (1964), WMU Distinguished Alumni Award (1970), Distinguished Alumni Award of the Association of State Colleges and Universities (1981), Michigan Women's Hall of Fame (1991) and American Historical Association Award for Scholarly Distinction (1991). She also established endowments at Western Michigan University, Radcliff College and Harvard University.

Merze died on June 27, 1996, at the age of ninety-one. She was buried in Pine River Cemetery in Blanchard, alongside members of her family. The local library in Blanchard was renamed the Tate Memorial Library in July 2014.

MICHAEL NICHOLSON

M ost people can't wait to escape the classroom and step out into the real world. But for one dedicated individual, the passion for academia led to a lifetime of learning at the collegiate level.

Michael Nicholson was born in 1941 in Highland Park, Michigan, to William and Nettie (Senchuk) Nicholson. His father made it through only third grade, and his mom graduated from high school but never furthered her studies beyond that. The ever-curious and ambitious Michael had a larger vision when it came to his professional education—much larger!

After graduating from Detroit Redford High School in 1959, Michael enrolled at Detroit Bible College. There, he met Sharon Nichols from Southfield, and the two were married in 1966. They both earned bachelor of religious education degrees (BREs), Michael in 1963 and Sharon in 1964.

From there, the newlyweds moved to Texas, where Michael earned a master's degree at the Dallas Theological Seminary (majoring in systematic theology) in 1967. Michael says this degree was his most challenging, as he had to pass exams in two languages, Hebrew and Greek, and write his first master's thesis.

Back in the Great Lakes State, Michael enrolled at Eastern Michigan University (EMU) in Ypsilanti, receiving a master of arts degree in classroom teaching in 1969 and a specialist in arts degree in 1970. Next came the University of Ottawa in Canada, where he earned a master's degree in school counselling in 1974.

The Nicholsons arrived in Kalamazoo in 1974, when Michael first enrolled at Western Michigan University (WMU), where he received a specialist in education degree in 1975, a doctor of education degree in 1977 and a master of business administration degree in 1978.

In the 1980s, Michael crisscrossed the state, racking up degrees, including a master's in library science from Wayne State University in 1980; an

Author's collection.

associate's degree in applied science (with a major in law enforcement) from Kalamazoo Valley Community College in 1982; an associate's degree in business from Lansing Community College in 1986; and a master's degree with a major in adult and continuing education from Michigan State University in 1988.

Nine of Michael's next ten master's degrees were earned at WMU, including majors in special education, 1990; reading, 1991; career and technical education, 1992; home economics, 1994; teaching in elementary school, 1995; teaching in middle school, 1996; early childhood education, 1997; human resources development, 1998; and physical education, 1999. In the middle of all that, he also earned a specialist's degree in school psychology from EMU (1993).

Michael made his way to Indiana University (IU) South Bend for his master of science degree in education in 2001, followed by his master of education degree in special education from Oakland University, 2003; and then back to IU for a master of science degree in education (secondary education), 2004. His last five master's degrees came from Grand Valley State University, including majors in education, 2005; public administration, 2008; health administration, 2009; special education administration, 2010; and criminal justice, 2014.

Over the course of fifty-five years, Michael earned thirty degrees (three specialist's, two associate's, one bachelor's, twenty-three master's and one doctorate) from twelve different institutions in three states and two countries. He was eighteen when he first started college and seventy-three when he earned his final degree. He walked in twenty-nine of his thirty graduation ceremonies and proudly displays his collection of graduation tassels in his home office.

So, how did Michael pay for all these degrees? For eleven years, he worked as a parking enforcement officer at WMU. He held several positions in education, including as a fifth grade teacher, high school counsellor and substitute teacher. He also worked as a newspaper carrier, factory worker and security guard to cover tuition expenses. He admits he wasn't an all-A student and couldn't have achieved this academic success without Sharon, who herself has earned seven degrees and worked in IT for WMU for thirty-eight years, retiring in 2017.

SECTION 4

SCIENCE, RELIGIOUS AND CIVIC FIGURES

NATHAN MACY THOMAS

The Michigan Freedom Trail Commission estimates that forty-five thousand escaped enslaved people made their way through Michigan to Canada during the 1800s. There were nearly three dozen confirmed Underground Railroad stations in Michigan, and one of the most well-known was the Schoolcraft home of Kalamazoo County's first physician.

Nathan Macy Thomas was born to North Carolina Quakers and abolitionists Jesse and Avis (Stanton) Thomas in Mount Pleasant, Ohio, on January 2, 1803. On his mother's side, he was a descendant of Thomas Macy, the second leader of the settlement of Nantucket Island. At the time of Nathan's birth, approximately eight hundred Quaker families were living in eastern and southern Ohio, and by 1814, that number had more than doubled. This religious sect, which made its way to Michigan in the early 1820s, was key to the advancement of the Underground Railroad and freedom for the enslaved.

After attending a series of schools in Mount Pleasant, Nathan taught briefly in Zanesfield in Logan County before returning home. In early May 1825, he began the study of medicine with Dr. Isaac Parker, who had come to Mount Pleasant seventeen years earlier. Nathan later attended the Medical College of Ohio (later called the College of Medicine of the University of Cincinnati), and in the spring of 1828, he completed his studies and was presented a certificate of membership to the Ohio Medical and Philosophical Society, according to his diary, which was donated to The Michigan Historical Collections at the University of Michigan.

By 1833, Dr. Nathan Thomas had moved north to Schoolcraft, Michigan, the first town in Kalamazoo County, founded on October 5, 1831. There, he established a medical practice and constructed a single-story rectangular building, described as a Greek Revival–style structure

Kalamazoo Public Library.

with Federal-style elements, on the northeast corner of Cass and Centre Streets, which served as his office (front) and residence (back).

He later met Permelia "Pamela" Smith Brown of nearby Prairie Ronde Township, and they were married on March 17, 1840. Between 1842 and 1857, they had four children (two boys and two girls), which necessitated expanding their small home, with the addition of wing sections on each end measuring twelve and a half feet wide by forty-two feet deep.

The larger house also allowed the Thomases to accommodate the growing number of escaped enslaved people who found temporary refuge behind their closed doors. It is said these fleeing individuals—sometimes a dozen at a time—were often brought by Zachariah Shugart in nearby Cass County. From there, Nathan would shuttle them to Battle Creek, where they made their way, station by station, to Detroit and ultimately Canada.

"His antislavery views were so well known, that, while he was a bachelor boarding at the hotel, fugitives from slavery had called on him for assistance and protection," Pamela wrote in her memoirs in 1892.

It is estimated that over a twenty-year period (from 1840 to 1860), the Thomases helped as many as 1,500 freedom seekers by providing them lodging, medical treatment, homecooked meals and transportation.

In 1845, Nathan ran unsuccessfully for lieutenant governor of Michigan on the Liberty Party ticket with James G. Birney, who bid for governor. Nathan was a key participant in the 1854 antislavery convention in Jackson and was a nominating committee member of the Michigan Republican Party.

Shortly after the Civil War, Nathan had his frame house moved across Grand Steet (present-day US-131) to 613 East Cass Street and erected a three story, four-thousand-square-foot brick Italianate home on his original property. The 1835 home was purchased by the Schoolcraft Historical Society in 1975 and restored, including the reconstruction of a previously demolished wing. It was added to the National Register of Historic Places in 1982, and today, it operates as the Underground Railroad House Museum.

Dr. Thomas died on April 7, 1887, at the age of eighty-four. He was buried in the Schoolcraft Township Cemetery, alongside Pamela, who passed away on January 28, 1909, at the age of ninety-two.

URIAH UPJOHN

There are a handful of families who have become synonymous with Kalamazoo due to their early business development, community leadership and longstanding philanthropic initiatives. Among them are the Upjohns, who first arrived in the early nineteenth century before Michigan even became a state.

Reverend William and Mary (Standard) Upjohn were married on March 14, 1796, in the United Kingdom, and over their marriage, they raised twelve children. Their ninth child was Uriah, who was born on September 7, 1808.

In April 1828, twenty-year-old Uriah and his older brother William (born on March 4, 1807), left for America and arrived in New York two months later. Together, the brothers enrolled in the College of Physicians and Surgeons, graduating in the 1830s. Since their time at the college, it has become the medical school at Columbia University.

In search of new opportunities, the brothers made their way to the Michigan Territory, crossing Lake Erie by steamer and landing in Detroit in June 1835. From there, they rode on horseback to Kalamazoo County, where Uriah acquired land in Richland Township and built a small cabin, while William settled a bit north in present-day Hastings in Barry County.

Uriah soon met Maria Mills, the daughter of one of the early pioneers, Deacon Simeon Asa Mills, and his wife, Clarissa (Porter), and they were married on September 15, 1837. The first of their twelve children was born within two years, thus planting familial roots that remain grounded in Kalamazoo to this day.

As a country doctor, Uriah covered a five-county territory, traveling by horseback through the undeveloped wilderness. His saddlebag was packed with homemade splints and bandages, surgical instruments, small scales

Uriah Upjohn, undated (series 4, box 6, folder 40); The Donald Reid Parfet/Upjohn Company Collection, privately held, Kalamazoo, MI.

and a mortar and pestle that he used to mix his own herbal medicines. A student of nature, he gathered plants along his route to make natural remedies for common ailments. He was also one of the first doctors to administer quinine as a treatment for pneumonia or malaria, which was prevalent in Michigan at the time.

During the 1860s, in addition to caring for his own patients, Uriah covered for his brother William, who was serving with the Union during the Civil War, first as a surgeon to the Seventh Michigan Cavalry and then rising to become surgeon-in-chief of the First Brigade, First Division, Cavalry of the Army of the Potomac.

Over time, six of Uriah's children followed in his medical footsteps (with five attending the University of Michigan). Mary and Amelia were among the university's first female graduates, both earning degrees in pharmacy. Helen, Henry, James and William all became physicians.

The greatest family legacy is attributed to Drs. Henry and William, who founded the Upjohn Pill and Granule Company in 1886. After Henry's death from typhoid fever in early 1887, William continued to lead the company until his own passing in 1932. The Upjohn Company merged with the Swedish company Pharmacia in 1995, forming Pharmacia & Upjohn. Upon its acquisition of Monsanto in 2000, the company changed its name to simply Pharmacia, which was acquired by Pfizer in 2003. As one of Kalamazoo's largest employers and Pfizer's single largest pharmaceutical plant, the Kalamazoo site was celebrated with the production and launch of the world's first COVID-19 vaccine following its approval in late 2020.

Outside of the medical world, Uriah was active with the Anti-Slavery Society, was nominated for Congress on the Free-Soil ticket in 1845 and joined the Republican Party when it formed in 1854. In 1862, William and Uriah also sent a petition to the legislature, supporting the passage of the Homestead Law.

Maria died at the age of sixty on February 17, 1882. Uriah lived until the age of eighty-eight, passing away November 23, 1896. At the time of his death, he was the oldest practicing physician in the county, having served nearly sixty years. The couple was buried in Kalamazoo's Mountain Home Cemetery, along with more than two dozen members of the Upjohn family.

SISTERS OF ST. JOSEPH

Since first arriving in Kalamazoo more than a century ago, the Sisters of St. Joseph have ministered to those in need, whom they call "the dear neighbor," in hospitals, schools, churches and social service organizations and agencies, many of which they founded to serve unmet needs.

The story of the Sisters of St. Joseph traces back to Le Puy, France, when six women with common spiritual and charitable goals formally organized in 1650. Nearly two centuries later, seven sisters from this congregation journeyed to America. Throughout the 1800s, seven communities organized around the country to aid in various humanitarian efforts. One of those groups made its way to Michigan at the request of the Diocese of Detroit and Monsignor Francis O'Brien of St. Augustine Parish in Kalamazoo.

In 1888, no hospital existed in Kalamazoo, but thanks to a $5,000 donation by Bishop Caspar Henry Borgess (the former bishop of Detroit), that was about to change. On March 5, 1889, the former Portage Road home of James A. Walter was purchased and converted into the first Borgess Hospital. Four months later, eleven women arrived in town from New York to form the Sisters of St. Joseph of Nazareth. Their first assignment was to operate this new medical facility, which was dedicated on October 13, 1889.

Twelve years later, the sisters planned a great celebration to commemorate the laying of the cornerstone for a hospital expansion. Trains brought dignitaries and parishioners to town on Sunday, June 10, 1901, for the parade that marched from the old St. Augustine on West Kalamazoo Avenue to the hospital about a mile away. For nearly three decades, the Sisters managed the Portage Road hospital until they purchased forty acres on Gull Road for a new, larger, modern, fireproof hospital. The March 19, 1916 issue of the *Kalamazoo Gazette* noted the site "is one of the finest locations for a hospital that can be mentioned near the city."

Construction soon began, and the following spring, the Sisters began their fundraising campaign to furnish patient rooms.

"The benefactors may select furniture, with the exception of the beds which the hospital reserves the right to purchase, so as to have them of proper design and efficiency," notes an April 22, 1917 *Kalamazoo Gazette* article. "The benefactor's name will

Courtesy of Congregation of St. Joseph Archives.

appear on the door of each room. The furnishing of a room does not mean that the benefactor will have the right to say who may be its occupant."

The new Borgess Hospital opened during the summer of 1917, and on Monday, September 17, the Sisters extended an invitation to Kalamazoo mayor James B. Balch and the city council to tour the facilities.

In addition to the hospital, the Sisters established their motherhouse at Nazareth on the outskirts of town on Gull Road, about a mile and a half east of the new hospital. They ran an orphanage, and in 1897, they opened Nazareth Academy, a school for girls, with the boys' Barbour Hall opening in 1902.

Nazareth College opened in 1912, was chartered in 1924 and first admitted men in 1971. By the late 1980s, the private liberal arts institution offered twenty-three undergraduate majors and two graduate programs. Yet declining enrollment and growing financial concerns led to its closure in 1992.

After efforts to establish a historic district to protect and preserve the complex failed, the administration building and library were torn down in 1995 and 1996, respectively, followed by the aged motherhouse and four other structures in 2020. The iconic stone wall, which spans Gull and Nazareth Roads and was constructed in part by Laverne Harman (see pages 94–95) in the late 1920s, still stands. As part of their commitment to the environment and care of creation, the Sisters in Kalamazoo donated a sixty-acre parcel adjacent to their property, known as Bow in the Woods, to the Southwest Michigan Land Conservancy for a public preserve.

For more on the congregation of St. Joseph, visit csjoseph.org.

FRANK HENDERSON

Toward the end of the nineteenth century, memberships in fraternal organizations and secret societies (Freemasons, Odd Fellows, Knights of Columbus, Shriners and Rotary) were growing at a rapid pace in the country, with as much as 40 percent of the adult male population belonging to at least one association. Led by esteemed members of the community, these groups were founded on tradition and ceremony, complete with uniforms, swords, hats, flags and other regalia. One local leader built his empire on these institutions and the customs with which they operated.

Frank Henderson was born in Syracuse, New York, in 1841 to Levi Sylvanus and Carissa (Amidon) Henderson. Ten years later, the family (three sons and two daughters) moved to Cass County, Michigan, where they set up farming operations and the children attended public schools in Dowagiac. At the age of nineteen, an entrepreneurial Frank moved to Kalamazoo, where he formed the Henderson & Brown Company with Charles Brown, specializing in hardware and saddlery.

On May 27, 1868, Frank married Mary Taylor, the daughter of James and Helen (Gilkison) Taylor. James's brother was George Taylor, a noted farmer and the individual responsible for Michigan's rich celery-growing industry (see pages 40–41). The Hendersons welcomed their first of six children (and only son) in 1869.

A few years into their business partnership, Brown retired, leaving Frank as the sole proprietor. He then began adding uniforms and regalia to his inventory. He later teamed up with T.F. Giddings in a short-lived partnership that left Giddings with the saddlery business and Frank with the regalia division.

Soon, Frank set out to erect a family estate to substantiate his growing fame and fortune, hiring surveyors, engineers and landscape architects to

Courtesy of Michigan Mason Museum and Library.

turn an elevated plot of land into a palatial abode. The twenty-five-room Queen Anne–style "castle" was constructed with a Lake Superior sandstone and brick façade, with a blend of mahogany, bird's eye maple, quartered oak, birch and American sycamore throughout the inside. It was completed in 1895 for $72,000 (over $2.6 million today).

In the 1890s, Frank established his final business partnership when he consolidated with the Chicago branch of the Ames Sword Company to form the Henderson-Ames Company. The business was so well respected it was recognized for excellence of quality and design at the 1893 Columbian Exposition in Chicago.

Frank himself was an active member of many groups, serving as a thirty-third-degree Freemason and one-time grand commander of the Knights Templar. He was involved with the Knight of Pythias, Odd Fellows, Elks, Ancient Order of United Workmen and the National Union. He belonged to several insurance orders, was affiliated with the Presbyterian Church (including lending his deep bass voice to the St. Luke's choir), served on the local board of education and was a two-term city trustee. He was president of Cosmopolitan Club, past president of the Kalamazoo Club and had served as secretary, treasurer and trustee of the Kalamazoo Gun Lake Fishing Club. He was also a director of the City National Bank, treasurer for the Kalamazoo Natural Gas and Fuel Company and was a stockholder in several enterprises, including the Bardeen Paper Company, the American Playing Card Company and the Kalamazoo Corset Company.

In March 1896, Frank suffered a stroke from which he never fully recovered. He passed away on January 3, 1899, at the age of fifty-seven. Mary lived until the age of sixty-one, passing away on July 26, 1907. Both are buried in Mountain Home Cemetery, across West Main Street from their beloved castle, along with other members of the Taylor and Henderson families.

Henderson Castle (HendersonCastle.com) operates as a twelve-guest-room boutique bed-and-breakfast, complete with a French-inspired restaurant, lounge, winery and spa. Popular for special events, the inn offers high tea, as well as guided tours of the building and grounds. It was listed for sale in early 2024.

Henderson-Ames regalia remains coveted by collectors and can be found at antique shops and online.

HOMER STRYKER

Doctors, nurses and patients at hospitals around the world have been using a variety of medical tools and rehabilitation equipment invented and perfected by an industrious doctor whose family legacy is one of the strongest in Kalamazoo.

Homer Hartman Stryker was born in Athens, Michigan (Calhoun County), on November 4, 1894, to Abraham Vincent and Eva L. (Hartman) Stryker. He attended Athens High School, where he was a member of the glee club, played on the baseball team and graduated in 1913.

From there, he was off to Western State Normal College (Western Michigan University), where he was active with the Hickey Debating Club, serving as fall president during his junior year; the Dramatic Association, portraying Mr. Tompsett in the presentation of *The Admirable Crichton*; contributing to the *Brown & Gold* yearbook; and participated in both track and reserve football. He graduated in 1916 and was off to the Keweenaw Peninsula in the wilds of Michigan's Upper Peninsula, where he taught one year in a one-room schoolhouse.

In late 1917, Homer joined the 107th U.S. Engineers, American Expeditionary Forces Company C, part of the Thirty-Second "Red Arrow" Division with units from the Michigan and Wisconsin National Guard, serving as a private in France and Germany during World War I. Thankfully, the war ended within a year.

After returning home, Homer applied to the University of Michigan Medical School. Lacking the proper foreign language requirements, his admission was delayed. Not deterred, he sought the help of a tutor, a teacher of German and French named Mary Jane Underwood, who had also graduated from Athens High School, where she was the valedictorian of her class and the first woman from her high school to attend college (Northwestern University in 1916). With her help, Homer passed his medical

Zhang Collection, Western Michigan University Archives.

school exam; now, he just needed money for tuition. He took a teaching and coaching position in Grand Ledge, while he also played baseball for a semi-pro team there.

Homer began his formal medical school studies in 1921, while maintaining his active lifestyle as a starting pitcher for the college's baseball team, even leading them to a Big 10 title in 1923. After graduating, he interned at University Hospital in Ann Arbor before working briefly at a small private hospital in Alma. He landed in Kalamazoo in 1928 and established a medical office on the second floor of the newly opened State Theater on South Burdick, serving as Kalamazoo County physician in 1929 and 1930.

In addition to starting his medical career, Homer picked up the title of husband and father. On June 24, 1924, he married his former tutor, Mary Jane, who wore "a charming gown of white silk crepe trimmed with Chantilly lace" and "carried a shower bouquet of swansonia, sweet peas and sweetheart roses," according to the *Lansing State Journal*. The couple had two sons, Homer Frederick (1928–1934) and Lloyd Lee (1930–1976).

Wishing to specialize his practice, Homer returned to the University Hospital for a residency in orthopedic surgery. It was here that he began developing equipment that would aid doctors, nurses and patients in dealing with mobility issues. In 1946, he formed the Orthopedic Frame Company, which evolved into today's global $9 billion Stryker Corporation. Among his noted inventions are the wedge turning frame, Circ-O-Lectric hospital bed, walking heel and cast cutter.

In 1968, Homer was awarded the Presidential Citation for Meritorious Service from the President's Committee for Employment of the Handicapped. Two years later, he was honored with the WMU Distinguished Alumni Award. Several Kalamazoo medical buildings and educational facilities bear the Stryker name, as does the Homer Stryker Field minor league baseball stadium, which celebrates his passion for the sport (home of the Jack Moss Press Box, see pages 108–109).

Homer Stryker died on May 5, 1980, at the age of eighty-five. He was buried in Burr Oak Cemetery in Athens, alongside Mary Jane, who also died in 1980.

CARRELLA (CLAY) PETERSON

For two decades, a Native woman set up camp in northern Kalamazoo County, utilizing skills she learned from her father to provide services and entertainment to many who traveled from near and far.

Little is known about the early life of the woman known as *Princess Red Feather*, a moniker shared with at least one—but perhaps two—other women of the era, causing confusion and inaccuracies in the reporting of her true family heritage. It is believed that Carrella (sometimes printed Corrella, Carella and Caerella) was born on June 1, 1890, in Oklahoma, the daughter of a famous Cherokee medicine man.

Carrella was first married at the age of seventeen (around 1907), according to the 1930 census, and it is believed she moved to Michigan with her unnamed husband. According to the Kalamazoo Valley Museum, Carrella found herself in northern Cooper Township in 1925, settling along old US-131, the former plank toll road that operated between 1852 and 1868 to connect Kalamazoo and Grand Rapids. Among her neighbors was a man named Arthur Oscar Peterson, known as Wild Horse Pete, who lived there with his brothers, Frank and Herman.

Princess Red Feather established a tourist camp on the west side of the road, and from the nearby woods, she would gather bark, plants, wild herbs and other elements that she would then mix into over three hundred remedies to cure ailments like a sour stomach, rheumatism, impure blood and tired, lazy feelings. She advertised in the local newspapers as early as 1926, providing seasonal hours of when she was at the camp, as she also traveled throughout the region offering her services.

Travelers could easily find Princess Red Feather's camp, as she had erected a large teepee and totem pole out by the road. She later opened a restaurant called Red Feather Inn with rabbit and chicken dinner specials, along with

Ransom District Library.

orchestra dancing on Saturday nights. Around 1929, Pete constructed thirteen small cabins for those who came from as far as three hundred miles to be treated by this medicine woman or to take in various stage shows and feats of magic.

After about fifteen years in Southwest Michigan, the Princess and her Pete moved out west (along with his brother Frank's four kids, whom they adopted) and took up with the Tom Mix Troupe. The 1940 census showed them living in Phoenix, Arizona, with her identified as a white woman with his last name. The union was likely common law, as they weren't officially hitched until April 5, 1948. The official license provided Corrella's date of birth as noted previously, along with her maiden name, Corrella R. Clay, and her location of birth, Calique, Oklahoma (which doesn't appear to be the name of an actual town).

The legal marriage was short-lived. Just over five months later, Pete died on September 28, 1948, of congestive heart failure. He was just fifty-seven years old, having been born in Chicago on December 1, 1890, to Swedish immigrants Edna and Charles Peterson. He broke horses for the army during World War I, which is how he earned his nickname. His obituary noted he was at one time a member of Buffalo Bill's Wild West Show, and until his death, he was often seen dressed in a cream-colored, fringed buckskin suit, cowboy hat and boots to go along with his shoulder-length hair and goatee.

After Pete's death, Carrella moved to Roswell, New Mexico, but it isn't known where or when she died or where she is buried.

Princess Red Feather's former restaurant building still stands at 9489 Douglas Avenue in Plainwell (northern Kalamazoo County), although it has been reincarnated over the years. In the late 1950s, it became The Ceramic Inn, a restaurant and later art studio, and then it became an apartment. At the time of this publication, it houses The Vintage Warehouse Estate Services.

ETTA FAIRCHILD

More than 235 years after the paranoia of witchcraft ripped through Salem, Massachusetts, an elderly Kalamazoo woman was accused of practicing dark acts, which ultimately led to her tragic murder at the hands of a radical husband-and-wife duo.

Laura Etta Runyan was born in April 1853 to John and Laura (Church) Runyan. Little is known about her early life, although according to the 1880 census, the twenty-six-year-old woman was a music teacher living in Genesee County, Michigan, with her parents.

On July 3, 1884, Etta married Madison French Fairchild in Wayne County, with his father officiating. Madison was the son of Gershom and Electa Bird (Runyan) Fairchild; his mother and Etta's father were siblings. The cousin newlyweds lived briefly in Genessee County before relocating to Kalamazoo in 1886. According to the 1902 Kalamazoo City Directory, they were residing at 1044 Sherwood Avenue, where they lived until Madison died of a heart attack on August 17, 1904, at the age of sixty-three.

Etta, who never had children or remarried, continued to live in the Sherwood Avenue home until the 1920s. Among her neighbors were Eugene and Pearl Burgess and their two children, Burnett and Eugenia, whom Etta had known for over fifteen years.

By 1925, due to her age and health, Etta had moved into the D.B. Merrill Home for Elderly Women near the corners of Lovell and South Westnedge Streets. A matron there described her as having a small, slight and stooped build; she had excellent eyesight but was reportedly deaf. A religious woman, Etta was known for her "refinement, gentleness and happy disposition." She was also considered a wonderful storyteller with a vivid imagination, especially as her mental capacities began to diminish.

The Burgesses had also moved. On July 18, 1929, they invited their seventy-six-year-old former neighbor to join them for dinner at their house

From True Detective Mysteries *magazine (April 1930).*

at 429 Ransom Street, about a mile away. Instead of serving Etta a meal, Eugene delivered a series of blows to her head with a lead pipe and a hammer, causing her brutal death. The couple then rolled up Etta's body in their bedding, curtains and dining room rug, tied everything together with electrical wire, attached a cement block and dumped everything in a backyard cistern.

Pearl shared details of the dastardly deed with neighbor Marian C. Ring, who immediately called the authorities with the grisly news. When police arrived at the Burgess home around 10:00 p.m., they found little had been done to clean up the crime scene—the walls, floors and furniture were bloodstained, as depicted in crime scene photos published in the April 1930 issue of *True Detective Mysteries* magazine. After the body was recovered from the cistern, it was sent to the coroner for examination. Etta's death certificate read "fracture skull murder." She also suffered nine broken ribs and two shattered arms.

What possessed fifty-one-year-old Pearl and fifty-four-year-old Eugene to execute such a vicious act? The two were religious fanatics, former members of the Christian Science Church and followers of the "Higher Thought" cult. They believed that Etta was a witch, responsible for the illness and deaths of hundreds of people, and they feared for their lives.

With confessions in hand, police charged the Burgesses with Etta's senseless murder. Eugene escaped persecution by hanging himself in his jail cell on September 29, 1929. Pearl faced a jury of her peers, and on October 18, 1930 (fourteen months to the day after the crime), she was found guilty of first-degree murder. The verdict was ultimately set aside when she was declared mentally unfit and institutionalized at the Ionia Hospital for the Criminally Insane. The 1950 census showed a seventy-year-old Pearl living with her daughter in Augusta; she died on May 15, 1970, at the age of ninety.

Etta and Madison were both interred in Kalamazoo's Riverside Cemetery. The original handwritten trial records, bound in oversized leather volumes, are kept in the archives at the Zhang Legacy Collections Center at Western Michigan University.

AUTHORS, ARTISTS AND COLLECTORS

JAMES FENIMORE COOPER

In 1992, Daniel Day-Lewis starred in the film *The Last of the Mohicans*, based on the 1826 novel written by one of America's premier historical novelists. More than two decades later, this famed author made his way to Michigan, where a visit to Prairie Ronde (present-day Schoolcraft) left an indelible impression and led to the publication of *The Oak Openings* in 1848.

Born in Burlington, New Jersey, on September 15, 1789, James Fenimore Cooper was the second youngest of eleven children (half of whom died in infancy) of Elizabeth (Fenimore) and William Cooper. When James was just a baby, his family moved to New York State, where his father had founded the village of Cooperstown on a large parcel of land he had purchased. It would become the seat of Otsego County, which was established on February 16, 1791. The family lived in a large Federal-style manor house called Otsego Hall, one of the largest private homes in central New York at the time. It was a fitting home for William, who was a judge and, later, a U.S. congressman, until his passing in 1809.

Sources say James lived an entitled life and, as a thirteen-year-old, was enrolled at Yale University, but his time there was short-lived. A perpetual prankster, he was expelled in his third year after a series of shenanigans. He then found work as a sailor, and by 1811, he was a midshipman in the U.S. Navy. That year, he also married Susan Augusta de Lancy, and they would go on to have seven children.

James began his professional writing career at the urging of his wife, and in 1820, his first novel, *Precaution*, was published anonymously (originally accredited to an English woman) by A.T. Goodrich. The next year, *The Spy* catapulted his reputation as a significant American writer under the name James Cooper. It wasn't until 1826 that he formally added his mother's surname, and from then onward, he was known as James Fenimore Cooper.

Public domain.

In 1833, Sarah Sabina Cooper, the daughter of James's older brother Isaac, married General Horace Hawkins Comstock, one of the early residents in Kalamazoo County's newly founded Comstock Township. He donated land and built a school there in exchange for the township being named after him. Comstock, who was later elected as the first senator from Kalamazoo County, named Cooper Township for his wife's family (and also named the village Otsego in adjoining Allegan County after Otsego Lake, New York).

During the late 1830s and early 1840s, James made a handful of trips to Kalamazoo to visit his niece and General Comstock. While exploring the nearby rural countryside, he befriended Judge Bazel Harrison, Kalamazoo County's first white settler, who became the lead character in his 1848 novel *The Oak Openings* (also called *The Bee Hunter*) (see pages 26–27). Set in Schoolcraft, the story follows professional honey hunter Benjamin Boden (also known as Ben Buzz) and is regarded as the first book about beekeeping in American literature.

It is commonly believed but undocumented that James spent two weeks at Calvin Cutler White's lodging establishment in Gun Plain Township (just north of present-day Plainwell) working on this book. As the first brick building in the county, it was also one of the earliest businesses to welcome weary travelers on their way between Kalamazoo and Grand Rapids along the Old Plank Road. It was known by several names over the years, including The Old Red Brick, The Red Brick Tavern (from 1931 until the 1950s or 1960s) and The Red Brick Inn.

James died from sclerosis of the liver on September 14, 1851, one day shy of his sixty-second birthday. His body lay in state at Otsego Hall, with funeral services held at Christ Church and interment in the family plot in the adjacent Cooperstown graveyard.

Back in Kalamazoo County, the Cooper legacy lives on at Cooper Elementary School, the Cooper's Glen Auditorium at the Kalamazoo Nature Center and the Cooper's Glen Music Festival.

EDNA FERBER

Several noteworthy twentieth-century motion pictures were based on novels written by Pulitzer Prize–winning author Edna Ferber, including *Giant*, the 1956 epic western with Rock Hudson, Elizabeth Taylor and James Dean (his last film before his tragic death); *Showboat*, 1929, 1936 (with Irene Dunn) and 1951 (with Ava Gardner); and *Saratoga Trunk*, a 1945 historical romance starring Gary Cooper and Ingrid Bergman.

Edna Ferber was born in Kalamazoo, Michigan, on August 15, 1885, to Jacob Charles and Julia (Neumann) Ferber. Jacob, who had been born in Hungary, immigrated to the United States as a teenager and worked on the family farm before meeting and marrying Julia, who had emigrated from Germany first to Milwaukee and later moved to Chicago.

In 1880, the couple relocated to downtown Kalamazoo and lived at 103 West Lovell Street. Their daughter Fannie was born in 1882, and the following year the Ferbers purchased a large two-story house at 825 South Park Street. It was here that Edna was born, much to the dismay of her mother. It had been no secret that Julia desired a son, whom she intended to name Edward Victor Ferber. When Dr. Adolph Hochstein informed the new and dismayed mother that she had, in fact, given birth to another daughter, the baby's name was changed to Edna.

"I may as well break down and confess that I was born in Kalamazoo, Michigan, shortly before the turn of the nineteen hundreds," Edna wrote in her 1937 autobiography, *A Peculiar Treasure*. "Incidentally, there are no bronze tablets in my birthplace, either. I have immensely enjoyed having hailed from so improbable-sounding a place as Kalamazoo."

According to a January 1967 synopsis of Edna's life in *Literary Landmarks*, a Magna Carta Press publication, Jacob operated a dry goods store called Ferber's Popular Bazaar, which was first located at 109 Main Street and

later at 114–116 East Main Street (now known as Michigan Avenue). It was also noted that the Park Street home was sold in 1886, and the family moved to 323 Dutton Street before relocating back to Chicago in 1899 to live with Julia's parents. The Park Street property was later split into two lots in 1912, and some speculate the house, too, was divided, now sitting a few lots apart at 823 and 901 South Park Street.

The Ferbers moved from Chicago to Ottumwa, Iowa, before eventually landing in Appleton, Wisconsin, when Edna was twelve. After graduating from Ryan High School, the aspiring writer was hired as a reporter at the *Appleton Daily Crescent* for a salary of three dollars a week. She also wrote for *The Milwaukee Journal.*

In her lifetime, Edna published twelve novels, twelve collections of short stories or novellas and two autobiographies, as well as numerous plays and musical adaptations. Her fourth book, *So Big,* was published in 1924 and earned her a Pulitzer Prize in 1925, selling over 300,000 copies. The Chicago Jewish Historical Society notes she was the first Jewish person to win a Pulitzer. Edna was honored as one of "Twenty Outstanding Women of the Twentieth Century" at the 1965 New York World's Fair and was inducted into the Illinois Hall of Fame (2006), Michigan Women's Hall of Fame (2009) and Chicago Literary Hall of Fame (2013).

Edna never married or had any children. From 1939 until her mother's passing in 1949, she lived in an enormous six-thousand-square-foot stone mansion she had custom built in Easton, Connecticut, called Treasure Hill. She later returned to New York City, where she died of stomach cancer on April 16, 1968, at the age of eighty-two. She was cremated, and the location of her ashes is unknown.

In addition to her autobiographies, details about Edna can be found in the biography *Ferber: Edna Ferber and Her Circle,* published in 1978 by her grandniece author Julie Gilbert.

FLETCHER CHARLES RANSOM

The surname Ransom was well known throughout the Kalamazoo area, but it was a third-generation member of this family who created an artistic impression that extended beyond the state's borders and remains on display, even today.

The Ransom family first arrived in Kalamazoo in 1835, when Major Ezekial Ransom and his wife, Lucinda (Fletcher), settled in what was then called Bronson. Many of their twelve children also relocated here, some making their own marks on the town's history.

Oldest son, Epaphroditus, was appointed as an associate justice of the Michigan Supreme Court in 1837, the same year Michigan became a state; served as chief justice (1843–48); was elected as the seventh governor of Michigan (1848–50); and served as a Michigan state representative (1853–54).

Farnsworth Fletcher, the fifth child and second son born to Epaphroditus, was a local doctor, served as a Michigan representative for Kalamazoo County (1845–46) and was the father of three, with two sons who lived into adulthood: Charles A., for whom the Ransom District Library in Plainwell is named, and John Noyes, a farmer and prominent community member in Alamo Township, where he and his wife, Caroline (Hydorn), raised their four children. The oldest of these was Fletcher Charles Ransom, born on October 23, 1870.

As a child, Fletcher attended the District 2 Evergreen School (later called the Ransom School), located at the southwest corner of B Avenue and Ravine Road on land donated by his father. He went on to study at The Art Institute of Chicago (1892–93) and later attended the Academy of Fine Arts in New York City. While there, he operated a studio and reportedly shared an apartment with baseball legend Denton True "Cy" Young in Greenwich Village, a haven for creative types at the time.

Newspaper articles in 1898 were already referring to Fletcher as a "well-known artist," even though his career was just getting started. Among his

Public domain.

first projects was a commission by *Collier's Weekly* to draw images of soldiers embarking for Cuba during the Spanish American War.

Fletcher married Jessamine K. McDonald, a well-known opera singer and socialite, on June 29, 1899, and according to the 1900 census, they were living in Brooklyn with her parents. Within a year, they also welcomed their only child, Jessamine Noyes Ransom.

In the early 1900s, Fletcher illustrated several books written by political reformist David Graham Phillips, including a 1907 title, *A Second Generation*. In 1910, he authored and illustrated a book on satirical cartoons about Teddy Roosevelt titled *My Policies in Jungleland*. His 1915 baseball painting called *Yer Out* is regarded as his most valuable piece, selling in 2016 in an online auction for $48,000.

Throughout his career, Fletcher, who was a member of the Society of Illustrators and who was later listed in the *Who Was Who in American Art*, created pieces for *Scribner's Magazine, Harper's Magazine, Ladies' Home Journal, The Saturday Evening Post* and *Women's Home Companion*, as well as both Gerlach & Barklow and the Osborn Company.

Among Fletcher's most noted works was a series of calendars for the Chicago & Illinois Midland Railway Company, produced first in 1932, featuring President Abraham Lincoln. Not long after he started this project, he became ill and moved back to Michigan to live with his sister Fannie and her husband, Franklin James Scott, in their home at 277 West Allegan Street (M-89) in Plainwell. The barn behind their home became his studio, and nine of the Lincoln images were painted there. Years later, the railroad donated the original art to the Abraham Lincoln Presidential Library and Museum in Springfield, Illinois; several prints are also exhibited at Lincoln's New Salem Historical Park in Petersburg, Illinois.

Fletcher died at the age of seventy-three on May 2, 1943, in Plainwell and was buried in the Alamo Center Cemetery along with several members of his family. Fletcher's daughter died in 1950, followed by his wife in 1951, and they're both buried in Illinois. The Ransom District Library in Plainwell, which owns a large number of Fletcher's original prints, staged a public exhibit of his artwork in 1996.

DONALD O. BOUDEMAN

One man's fascination with historical artifacts led to a lifetime of collections, including one prominent item that is among the most treasured at the Kalamazoo Valley Museum.

Donald Oernst Boudeman was born in Kalamazoo on August 6, 1880, the middle son of Dallas and Mary Jane (Oernest) Boudeman. As a teen, he was a cadet at the Michigan Military Academy, an all-boys' military prep school on Orchard Lake in Oakland County, graduating on June 16, 1898. He attended one year at the University of Michigan, where he sang with the Freshman Glee Club, served on the Freshman Banquet Committee and pledged the Alpha Delta Phi fraternity. According to the 1900 census, Donald was a student living in Schenectady, New York.

On July 24, 1901, Donald applied for a passport and was soon off to Europe. While his purpose for the trip is unknown, he was still there in the fall of 1902, when the *Kalamazoo Gazette* ran an article noting his parents were setting sail for Hanover, Germany, to take care of their ailing son.

Back in the United States, Donald married Mabel Hosking on May 20, 1905, at the Hyde Park Hotel in Chicago (one of the ushers was Albert Todd, see pages 42–43). That same year, Donald's father had a stately Georgian-Colonial home built at 515 West South Street in Kalamazoo, where Donald lived out his life. In 1911, he and Mabel welcomed their only son, Donald Jr., although that marriage ended in divorce in late 1917. A year and a half later, Donald married a local antiquarian, Donna L. Nicholson.

An insurance salesman by day, Donald began collecting historical pieces, specifically Native relics, Egyptian artifacts, musical instruments, medieval armor, firearms, English porcelain and foreign currency and documents connected to European kings and queens, according to the Kalamazoo Valley Museum. He funded his hobby from an inheritance he received from

From the collection of the Kalamazoo Valley Museum.

his paternal grandfather, William Boudeman, who died in 1890.

Donald's most noted acquisition came in 1910, when he purchased a mummy from a private collector in California. It was brought to the United States in 1894 as part of a Cairo exhibit at the California Mid-Winter Exposition at San Diego's Golden Gate Park. Drawing more than two million people, the five-month event featured four major buildings spread out over two hundred acres. After the expo ended, the mummy remained on display in the Golden Gate Park Museum prior to Donald's procurement.

In Kalamazoo, Donald enlisted the help of a skilled surgeon armed with delicate instruments to remove the linen from the mummy's head while keeping the body fully wrapped, thus determining the body was female and about three thousand years old. Years later, in 1928, Donald donated the mummy to the Kalamazoo Public Museum on South Rose Street, where it became an instant attraction.

In 1948, the mummy was X-rayed to learn more about it. They found no jewels encased in its abdomen, something that likely would have been found had the woman been royalty. Additional noninvasive electronic scans of the mummy took place in 1988, and in 1989, it was even featured on an episode of *Reading Rainbow*. What they learned from these procedures was that the woman had died around the age of forty-five of apparent natural causes, given she had no broken bones or signs of trauma, although she likely suffered sinus issues and had poor dental hygiene.

Today, the mummy is permanently housed at the Kalamazoo Valley Museum (KalamazooMuseum.org), which moved to 230 North Rose Street in downtown Kalamazoo in 1996.

Donald Boudeman, who was active with the Michigan-Indiana Museums Association, including serving stints as the organization's vice-president from fall 1930 through early 1931, died on February 28, 1949, at the age of sixty-eight. Donna died in 1987, and the two were buried in Mountain Home Cemetery. The house on South Street was purchased by the W.E. Upjohn Institute for Employment Research, which remains active.

GWEN FROSTIC

One of Western Michigan University's most generous benefactors began her life struggling to make her way after a childhood illness left her with a limp, slurred speech and weak, crippled hands. Despite these lifelong challenges, she became one of America's most celebrated nature artists of all time with a successful Northern Michigan retail and mail-order business that she built from the ground up.

Sara Gwendolen Frostic was born on April 26, 1906, in Sandusky, Michigan, the second of nine children to Fred and Sara (Alexander) Frostic. She was about eight months old when a high fever nearly killed her, leaving her with lifelong symptoms similar to those of cerebral palsy. Throughout her childhood, her parents (both educators) encouraged her involvement in a variety of activities. She soon found an interest in art, teaching herself different methods and taking classes in mechanical drawing at Theodore Roosevelt High School in Wyandotte. She was even voted class artist and helped with all kinds of creative school projects.

After graduating in 1924, Gwen went on to study arts education at Michigan State Normal College in Ypsilanti (now Eastern Michigan University), earning a teacher's certificate and becoming a member of AΣT's first chapter. She later attended Western State Normal College in Kalamazoo (now Western Michigan University, or WMU).

For a brief period, Gwen operated a studio in her parents' basement before acquiring her first Heidelberg printing press and setting up shop in downtown Wyandotte, where her company, Presscraft Papers, was born.

During this era, she taught art classes at the Detroit WYCA and was even commissioned by Clara Ford (the wife of Henry Ford) to create one-of-a-kind pieces for Fair Lane, the Ford's family home in Dearborn. During World War II, Gwen worked her days at Ford's Willow Run bomber plant,

Gwen Frostic Studios.

dedicating her nights and weekends to her craft, which had transitioned from hard-to-acquire metal to linoleum block.

Over time, she would sketch everything from cranes and fireflies to wildflowers and sunsets on paper; then she would trace the image onto the back of a linoleum block (in reverse) and use her bent hands to carve those images into blocks using a blade or knife. These would later be attached to her printing presses and used to stamp ink onto the final items: stationery, napkins, booklets, calendars, mugs and a catalog of other collectibles.

In the 1950s, Gwen moved her operations to Benzie County, along the Lake Michigan shoreline, first to Frankfort and then to a wooded forty-acre plot in Benzonia, where she designed and built her landmark studio and gift shop. Tucked into the hillside, the nature-inspired structure features boulders, a stone fireplace, carved tree trunks and a natural spring fountain, which, today, encompasses over twenty-three thousand square feet with more than a dozen printing presses.

Regarded as one of Michigan's most noted environmentalists, nature artists, authors and lecturers, Gwen was honored with her own day in 1978, when then Michigan governor William Milliken proclaimed May 23 as Gwen Frostic Day in Michigan. Less than a decade later, she was inducted into the Michigan Woman's Hall of Fame, and during her lifetime, she received honorary degrees from five Michigan universities.

Gwen, who never married or had any children, died in her studio apartment on April 25, 2001 (the day before her ninety-fifth birthday). Upon her passing, she bequeathed $13 million to WMU—one of the largest single gifts in the university's history. The allocation of the unrestricted gift was left to college president Elson Floyd and the board of trustees, who ultimately chose to endow several scholarships and doctoral fellowships, as well as support environmental studies and creative writing, including the Gwen Frostic Reading Series. The donation was also used to help fund a new art facility, which was renamed the Gwen Frostic School of Art in 2007.

In the spring of 2020, Gwen Frostics Prints (GwenFrostic.com), which is still open seasonally, along with a year-round international mail-order business, was added to the National Register of Historic Places.

LAVERNE S. HARMAN

The use of stone in architecture dates to the origins of human civilization, with one the most famous rock formations, Stonehenge, built in approximately 2500 BCE. Throughout southeast Kalamazoo and northeast St. Joseph Counties, the legacy of one monumental stonemason remains proudly standing.

Caroline Magdalena (Reichert) and Harry Sylvester Harman raised their eight children in the Leonidas/Factoryville area in northern St. Joseph County. Their youngest was Laverne S., born on January 16, 1907. Little is known about the Harman family, but it is likely that the children attended the Leonidas Village School, built in 1859 for a mere $1,000.

At the age of seventeen, Laverne began working as an apprentice for stonemason Charles Blue of Mendon. One of his first projects was one of his most prominent, the six-foot-tall stone wall that surrounds the former Nazareth College campus at the intersection of Gull and Nazareth Roads (see pages 72–73). Reportedly earning just thirty cents an hour, Laverne helped craft the 2,600-foot Gull Road section using 119,000 stones (granite, gneiss, dolomite, porphyry, quartz and jasper) during the summers of 1928 and 1929. A different crew constructed the 1,600-foot stretch along Nazareth Road using 35,000 fieldstones. A marker built into the wall notes its reconstruction in 1983 by Bonnema Masonry, and although most of the buildings on the defunct campus were razed in 2019 and 2020, the wall and its grand entrance remain.

Laverne's next project took shape sixteen miles to the southeast in the village of Climax, where Michigan's first Rural Free Delivery (RFD) mail route was established on December 3, 1896. Willis Loomis "Willie" Lawrence served as the first rural carrier, earning forty-five dollars a month. It is said he used his own horse and buggy, or bicycle, and covered as many as thirty miles a day on unpaved country roads to deliver the mail. Along

Laverne Harman (*right*) pictured outside the Climax Post Office that he helped build in 1931. *Prairie Historical Society of Climax.*

the way, he collected farm field stones (seventy-five truckloads in all), which he and Laverne used to construct a new twenty-eight-foot-by-thirty-foot, one-story post office building at 107 North Main Street in 1931. The Lawrence family owned the building and rented it for a nominal fee to the U.S. Postal Service.

After Lawrence's death in 1934, his wife, Jette, maintained the governmental relationship until her passing in 1962. The building was then donated to the village, and two years later, it was dedicated as the Lawrence Memorial Library. In 1975, a 24-foot-by-24-foot English Tudor–style room was added to one side of the building, followed by a 1,300-square-foot Neo Greek Revival–style room constructed in back in 1990. In 1999, the stone building was added to the National Register of Historic Places, and today, it is also home to the Prairie Historical Society.

Laverne and Charles collaborated again when they broke ground on December 15, 1933, on a new sixty-foot-by-sixty-foot fieldstone schoolhouse in Leonidas, funded by President Roosevelt's New Deal Civil Works Administration. Others involved in the project were architect Wendall (or Randall) Wagner and carpenter Charles Robinson, along with a crew of eighteen who worked day and night to stay on schedule.

The *Battle Creek Enquirer* reported that the school was designed with sliding partitions between its four classrooms so that it could be opened into one large auditorium. It was also equipped with a basement, modern heating and ventilation systems and an oak-trimmed interior. District taxpayers funded the completion of the project, and the school finally opened in 1935. It has operated now for nearly nine decades and remains an active educational K-8 institution as part of the Colon Community School System.

Laverne married Ruth Gladys Halsey on March 17, 1928. They were married for fifty-seven years, with no known children, until his passing in 1985. In addition to the public spaces he constructed, Laverne (who retired in 1969) built two homes for Ruth and himself. They were buried in North Fulton Cemetery, along with her parents and several other members of the Halsey family.

SUE (GILBERT) HUBBELL

Individuality is the salt of common life" was the phrase published in the 1952 yearbook of the Western Normal High School next to the photograph of senior Suzanne Gilbert. During her life, this independent, self-reliant, strong-willed, creative and free-spirited woman set herself apart from the crowd and not only walked her own path but also carved it out with determination, wit and spunk.

Born on January 28, 1935, to B. Leroy and Marjorie (Sparks) Gilbert, Suzanne was the youngest of two children. Marjorie was a homemaker and later served in the Peace Corps. Leroy, a landscape architect, worked for the city of Kalamazoo as a parks commissioner, and he served briefly as city manager (1950–51). He was also a syndicated landscape columnist for the *Lansing State Journal* and the *Detroit Free Press*.

Sue attended Western Normal High School, where she was a member of the French Club, Bridge Club, Blue and Gold Revue, Student Council, Debate Team and Masquers drama program, and she contributed to the *Highlights* student newspaper and *Highlander* yearbook. She also served as homeroom vice-president and president before she graduated in 1952.

As a teenager, Sue met Paul Hubbell, a neighbor and student at nearby St. Augustine High School. She went on to study at Swarthmore College in Pennsylvania, and he studied at Western. But soon, they mutually agreed to transfer to University of Michigan in Ann Arbor to be together. They were married in 1955, and the next year, they moved to Los Angeles, where Paul worked for Douglas Aircraft and Sue finished her journalism degree at the University of Southern California, while also raising their newborn son, Brian.

The Hubbells later moved to Moorestown, New Jersey, where Sue managed a small bookstore and earned her master's degree in library science

Western Normal High School's 1951 yearbook.

from Drexel University in Philadelphia. She was then hired as an acquisitions librarian at Trenton State College, and when the family relocated to Providence, Rhode Island, she worked as a periodical librarian at Brown University.

In 1972, the family sold their house and set out in a modified Volkswagen microbus to travel the country as part of the back-to-the-land movement. They settled on a meager farm in the Ozark Mountains of Missouri, where beekeeping passed the time and paid (most of) the bills. It was here that Sue also began her freelance writing career, submitting articles to the *St. Louis Post-Dispatch* and, eventually, *The New York Times*.

The challenging country life led the couple to divorce in the early 1980s. Sue, who had become proficient in living frugally off the land, kept the farm (including three hundred hives) and expanded her writing to include deeply personal, gritty and often humorous essays and books. Her first memoir, *A Country Year: Living the Questions* (1983), shed light on the seasons of solo life for a mid-life woman in the Ozarks. *A Book of Bees* (1988), described as "a melodious mix of memoir, nature journal and beekeeping manual," was named a "Notable Book" by *The New York Times*.

By this time, Sue was spending her time between Missouri and Washington, D.C., and drawing acclaim for her writings. One of those reviews crossed the desk of Frank A. Sieverts, a former college friend of Sue's. He reached out, they met up and eventually, the two were married in 1988 (until his passing in 2004).

Sue went on to publish four other books: *On This Hilltop*, 1991; *Broadsides from Other Orders: A Book of Bugs*, 1993; *Far-Flung Hubbell: Essays from the American Road* (featuring two stories set in Michigan), 1995; and *Waiting for Aphrodite: Journeys into the Time Before Bones*, 1999. Her brother Bil began his career as a teenage reporter for the *Kalamazoo Gazette* and went on to become a world-traveler and freelance writer, living until 2012.

In 1996, Sue moved to Maine to be near her son and his wife, Liddy. She passed away there on October 13, 2018, at the age of eighty-three.

DONALD BONEVICH

A stint as a puppeteer on a locally produced children's television show was just one facet of a long-time teacher, painter, sculptor and stage actor's artistic career.

Donald Eugene Bonevich was born on February 1, 1928, in Canton, Ohio, to Frank and Anna (Temsic) Bonevich. He attended Lincoln High School, where he played football, basketball and baseball for the Lincoln Lions and was also vice-president of his sophomore class. After graduating in 1946, he received a scholarship to study sculpture at Carnegie Institute of Technology in Pittsburgh, and while he was there, he created a portrait sculpture honoring the memory of a World War II hero from his hometown. He then served in the U.S. Army, stationed in the Philippines.

Upon returning to America, Don worked briefly as a commercial sculptor before enrolling at the esteemed Art Institute of Chicago, where he earned a bachelor of arts in education degree in 1954. The next summer, he received a $750 graduate fellowship from Western Michigan University, which allowed him to work fifteen hours a week while doing graduate work. He earned his master of arts degree in 1956, and over the years, his various forms of artwork were displayed at galleries, auditoriums and shows in both Michigan and Chicago.

Settling into life in Kalamazoo, Don began teaching children's classes for the Gilmore Art Center, part of the Kalamazoo Institute of Arts, in 1957. He was also noted as being on the faculty at Western Michigan University, Kalamazoo College and Kalamazoo Public Schools. In the mid-1960s, he began a career as an art teacher at Portage Northern High School. On March 9, 1962, he married Ann Wiltse, and the couple later had three sons.

Outside of the classroom, Don was active with Kalamazoo's Actors and Playwrights Initiative and was a regular on the stages at Kalamazoo Civic Theatre, The New Vic Theatre, The Legend Theater at Sleepy Hollow

Donald Bonevich with his handmade puppets Mags and Lambert the Lion. *Portage Public Schools, Portage Northern High School's 1997 yearbook.*

Resort in South Haven and the Red Barn Theatre in Saugatuck, where he also designed sets. During his acting career, Don appeared in more than one hundred shows, including musicals, comedies and dramas, winning best actor awards at Michigan's Community Theatre Festival in 1999, 2001, 2004 and 2005. He also wrote and produced a show called *The Many Parts That I Have Played*, which features thirteen songs and was performed in 2005 with fellow actor B.J. Silverstone at The Legend Theatre.

Don was a treasured part of the lives of countless local children in the 1960s and 1970s. He hosted puppet shows and led puppet-making classes for kids during the summers at the Red Barn Theatre, calling himself the "Pied Piper of Puppets," with his handmade characters Lambert the Lion, Mags and Nigel.

His puppets were also an integral part of one of Kalamazoo's legendary kids' television programs: *Channel 3 Clubhouse.* Premiering on Tuesday, May 8, 1956, the thirty-minute show aired on WKZO (now WWMT-TV3) Monday through Friday at 5:00 p.m. In 1984, the show was reduced to just Saturdays and Sundays at 7:30 a.m. Over the course of thirty years, it is estimated that more than twenty-five thousand children appeared on the show, which also featured the occasional Disney character and beloved Captain Kangaroo, the star of a show that also aired on CBS on weekday mornings from 1955 to 1984. When the last episode of *Channel 3 Clubhouse* aired at 7:30 a.m. on Sunday, February 2, 1986, it was one of the nation's longest-running children's programs.

Don retired from Portage Northern in 1993, and in 2012, he received Canton Lincoln High School Distinguished Alumni and Lifetime Achievement Award. He and Ann continued to live in Kalamazoo until he passed away on May 12, 2019, at Rose Arbor Hospice at the age of ninety-one.

DONALD SHERWOOD GILMORE

After years of running two of Kalamazoo's most noted yet distinctly different companies, an ambitious community leader left a lasting legacy that has become one of the country's premier automobile museums.

Gilmore brothers John M. (born in 1852) and James F. (born in 1857) were among the seven children born in Northern Ireland to Samuel and Jane Gilmore. On May 7, 1879, John arrived in New York, followed by James five months later. John made his way to Michigan, where, in 1881, he opened a dry goods store on the west side of Burdick Street in downtown Kalamazoo. James arrived in 1883, prompting a move into a larger building across the street for what was to become the Gilmore Brothers Department Store.

On July 20, 1886, James married Carrie M. Sherwood, and they had three sons, including Donald Sherwood Gilmore, born on March 7, 1895. Just three months later, John died at the age of forty-two, leaving James the sole proprietor of the company until his own passing in 1908 at the age of fifty-one. James's widow assumed stewardship of the store and, as its chief executive, led the operation to new heights of commercial success. In 1913, she married her neighbor, widower William E. Upjohn.

Donald, who was also called "Prince" and "Gill," entered The Lawrenceville School, an independent college preparatory academy in New Jersey, in 1912. He was a member of the cross-country team (serving as captain in 1915), treasurer of the YMCA, vice-president of the Good Government Club, member of the Calliopean Society (a fraternity of Phi Epsilon Mu, a literary and debating organization), business manager of the *OLLA POD* yearbook, served on the Lit Board and was presented third prize in an essay contest during his junior year.

After graduating in 1916, Donald briefly attended Yale Sheffield Scientific School in New Haven, Connecticut, before returning to Kalamazoo to help

Donald Sherwood Gilmore, circa the early 1950s; (Photograph 0246); The Martha Gilmore Parfet and Ray Theodore "Ted" Parfet Jr. Collection, privately held, Kalamazoo, MI.

with the family business and marry Genevieve Upjohn, his stepsister. The next year, at the age of twenty-three, Donald was appointed to the Gilmore Brothers' board of directors. That fall, he and Genevieve welcomed the first of their three daughters, Carol. Their other daughters, Jane and Martha, arrived in 1919 and 1925, respectively.

Donald shifted careers in 1929, after his brother-in-law, Harold Upjohn, unexpectedly passed away. Harold had been running The Upjohn Company, and with his seat vacated, William E. Upjohn (Donald's father-in-law, who was also his stepfather) convinced the young man to join the company. Donald served in a variety of positions over the years, including chairman of the board and chief executive officer. During his tenure, he led its transition to a publicly traded company in the late 1950s.

Upon Donald's retirement in 1963, Genevieve presented him with a 1920 Pierce-Arrow, which he restored at his home on nearby Gull Lake. That gift sparked something in Donald and led him to collect rare and renowned vehicles, including a 1927 Ford Model T and a 1913 Rolls-Royce.

With a growing assemblage of automobiles, Donald acquired ninety acres of land in nearby Hickory Corners and began transforming the space into a one-of-a-kind attraction, which opened on July 31, 1966, as the Gilmore Car Museum (GilmoreCarMuseum.org). Today, this year-round complex displays over four hundred vehicles in more than 190,000 square feet of exhibit space. The grounds feature several historic barns, as well as a fully functioning 1941 Silk City Diner, a recreated 1930s Shell Service Station, six on-site partner museums and much more.

Donald died at the age of eighty-four on December 21, 1979, and Genevieve passed on March 12, 1990, at the age of ninety-five; they were buried in Mountain Home Cemetery. Their English-style country home on Short Road in Kalamazoo was gifted by their three daughters to Western Michigan University in 1991. The Gilmore Brothers Department Store closed in 1999 after more than a century of serving the local community.

SECTION 6

ATHLETES AND FANS

FLORA TEMPLE

At dawn of day they began to pour into town, on foot and on horseback, in heavy lumber wagons, in rickety go-carts, and in ponderous, double-down family turn-outs, each and all of which were filled with individuals of the one sex not only, but also of the other—gentler, but none the less enthusiastic."

Such was the scene on the morning of Friday, October 15, 1859, at the National Driving Park, according to an article that appeared days later in the *Kalamazoo Gazette* (sourced from the *Detroit Free Press*).

Built in 1858 on land purchased by the National Horse Association of Kalamazoo, led by U.S. senator Charles E. Stuart of Portage, the park was located between present-day Portage, Stockbridge, Cameron and Reed Streets in the Edison Neighborhood. The first exhibition race was presented here on October 15, 1858.

According to the United States Trotting Association, harness racing tracks began popping up around the country in the mid-1800s, although events had been held at county fairgrounds for decades. By the mid-twentieth century, harness racing, also known as trotting, was the fastest-growing sport in America.

One year to the day after opening, the park's most famous horse race occurred in front of a crowd of more than three thousand men, women and children, who filed into the grandstand two hours before post time so as to not miss a moment of the action. Among the horses on the docket were Honest Anse, Princess and Flora Temple, the favorite to win.

"Flora Temple was in the finest condition imaginable, her compact muscular form, and elastic step, and the fire of her brilliant eyes speaking volumes in favor of the fortunes of that, to her, eventful day," said the newspaper.

There are varying accounts of who sired Flora Temple with Madam Temple in 1845 in Utica, New York. Most sources attribute the honors to

Bogus Hunter (although One-Eyed Kentucky Hunter is also referenced). Either way, by the time she had arrived in Kalamazoo, Flora Temple was a national racing icon, considered the "Queen of the Turf."

She put on a royal show in Kalamazoo, setting a record time of 2:19.75 for the one-mile track, becoming just the second mare, after Lady Suffolk, to clock under 2:30 for a one-mile trot and making horseracing history (at the time). Not everyone was happy with the results, and many race fans on the East Coast were skeptical of the results coming out of an obscure place like Kalamazoo, with false claims that the track must have been less than a full mile in length, and for years, the controversy raged. A railroad surveyor eventually went to Kalamazoo to measure the track, finding it to be thirty inches longer than a mile, and with that, Flora Temple's record became official.

In her lifetime, Flora equaled or beat the record six times, even surpassing her own best times. By the time she retired in 1861, she had won 95 of her 112 events, and in 1955, she was inducted into the Harness Racing Hall of Fame as an "Immortal" for garnering at least 92 wins in her career.

After she left the track, Flora Temple was sent to the Erdenheim Stud Farm of Aristides Welce in Philadelphia, and at the age of twenty-four, she was bred to the imported Thoroughbred Leamington and birthed a foal named Prince Imperial. She died at the farm on December 21, 1877, and was buried there.

The last official horse race at Kalamazoo's National Driving Park occurred in 1886. During its twenty-eight-year history, the grounds were utilized as a Civil War training site and hosted the Michigan State Fair (1871 and 1872). Buffalo Bill's Wild West Show even set up its traveling act there in 1898. Around the turn of the century, a group of local investors turned the park area into the residential neighborhood that remains today.

THADDEOUS "TED" NOWAK

On the north side of Kalamazoo sits a historic bar where locals say everyone knows your name—including the name of the family who founded and ran this century-old institution.

Thaddeus "Ted" Nowak was born on June 6, 1915, the son of Polish immigrant Louis Nowak and his Russian-born wife, Mary (Males). The Nowaks lived in an area of town predominantly made up of Polish, Italian and German families, and in 1918, they opened a restaurant and soup kitchen at the corner of East North and Walbridge Streets called Louie's.

Prohibition was in effect in Michigan at that point, having been instituted on May 1, 1917 (three years before the national ban), but that didn't stop Louis and Mary from serving up bootleg liquor at Louie's. The July 31, 1921 issue of the *Kalamazoo Gazette* ran an article with the headline "Couple Seized in Booze Raid—Louis Nowak and His Wife Arrested: Officers Invade Home and Restaurant," and on September 6, the paper reported the couple was bound over to the grand jury to face charges. The last reference to this situation came on November 1 and noted that Louis had been indicted in federal district court in Grand Rapids, with no reference to the charges against Mary.

Growing up in the family business, Ted was serving as manager in 1939, when the Louie's Athletic Association Fund was established to sponsor various sports activities throughout the community. About this time, Ted and his wife, Louise (Malec), took over the operation of the restaurant. In between slinging burgers and beers, the second generation made an even greater impact on the local community.

Over the course of the next thirty years, Louie's name was emblazoned on a variety of sports teams for youth, men and women. Whether it was basketball, baseball, softball, golf or bowling, Ted had a personal interest

Courtesy of the Nowak family.

in creating opportunities for local residents to participate in these recreational activities.

His 1970 obituary started with the phrase, "There was never a better nor more enthusiastic friend of sports in Kalamazoo than Thaddeus S. (Ted) Nowak." The piece went on to say, "Ted was best known in sports circles for his sponsorship of championship teams.…Ted's teams, representing his Louie's Restaurant, won no fewer than 41 championship trophies over the years. Sponsorship of those teams, many of them during the depression years, gave a real boost to sports from both competitive and spectator aspects." It concluded, noting, "Ted Nowak, one grand guy, wrote an indelible chapter in Kalamazoo's sports history. There will never be another like him."

Throughout his lifetime, Ted also embraced his heritage and, in 1946, was named president of the Michigan Polish Bowling Association. Over a six-year period, Ted and his father were involved in the fundraising and building of a "Dom Polski," translated to mean "Polish Home," at 10 Mills Street in Kalamazoo. It was built by members of White Eagle Lodge 144 of the Polish National Alliance, of which Ted was president; Louis was chairman of the building committee. The $20,000 building was dedicated on Sunday, October 21, 1921.

After Ted's death on May 24, 1970, from heart disease, Louise, affectionately known as "Granny," continued to operate the family business. She was a loyal promoter of her Polish culture and for years celebrated Dingus Day at Louie's on the Monday after Easter, a holiday as significant to the Polish as St. Patrick's Day is to the Irish, according to a 1994 article by noted *Kalamazoo Gazette* writer Jack Moss (see pages 108–109).

Third-generation Louie Nowak (the grandson of Louis and one of seven children born to Ted and Louise) began working at the restaurant in the late 1960s, putting in nearly forty years before selling it in 2007 to longtime patron Mark Vandemaele of Mattawan. It has since been rebranded as Louie's Trophy House Grill (LouiesKzoo.com) but remains the oldest operating bar in Kalamazoo.

JACK NORRIS MOSS

One of the noted journalists at the *Kalamazoo Gazette* was more than a sports editor, he was what one colleague described as a "chronicler" of the city for more than five decades.

Jack Norris Moss was born in Kalamazoo on September 19, 1927, to Jack and Elsie Lorraine (Smeins) Moss. As a child, he listened to sports on the radio and dreamed of becoming a basketball coach. He attended Kalamazoo State High School, where they called him Modoc, and his first published piece was a class essay about the lack of school spirit. Jack was also a reserve player on the school's basketball team, and through a connection from a classmate, he became a *Kalamazoo Gazette* stringer covering the team on which he played.

After graduating in 1945, Jack advanced to Western Michigan University and became a sportswriter for *The Western Herald*. During his junior year, he dropped out and accepted a full-time position at the *Gazette*. It was a decision that changed his life forever.

Outside of a two-year period from 1950 to 1952, when he served in the U.S. Army during the Korean conflict, Jack's world centered on his hometown. On June 2, 1951, while on leave, he married Janet Marie Gardner of Middleville, and they would go on to have three children.

Jack was named the *Gazette*'s sports editor in 1967, a position he held until his retirement in 2002. During his esteemed fifty-three-year career, Jack covered local high school and Michigan college sports, thirteen Rose Bowls and countless other college bowl games, two Super Bowls, NCAA Men's and Women's Finals, three World Series, Wimbledon, the Kentucky Derby and multiple Indy 500 races, and while he wasn't working at the time, he attended the 1952 Olympics in Helsinki, Finland.

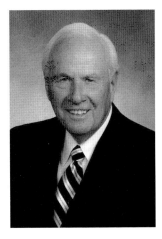

Michigan Sports Hall of Fame.

His career also introduced him to the who's who in the sports world, like Muhammad Ali, Joe Louis, Arnold Palmer, Magic Johnson, Jesse Owens, Bo Schembechler, George Steinbrenner and Derek Jeter (see pages 114–115), as well as four presidents: Eisenhower, Nixon, Ford and Reagan.

While Jack was the master of ceremonies at various functions, he often was the one being recognized such as in 1979 when he was inducted into the Michigan Media Hall of Fame or in 1998, when he received an honorary Doctor of Public Service degree from WMU. In 2005, he became the first sportswriter inducted into the Michigan Sports Hall of Fame.

His legacy lives on in the form of the Jack Moss Scholarship Fund—which provides $1,000 awards annually to area high school seniors (one male and one female) who plan to attend WMU, Kalamazoo College or Kalamazoo Valley Community College—and at Homer Stryker Field, you'll find the Jack Moss Press Box.

Regarded as one of the best sports writers in Michigan, Jack won nine Associated Press awards; helped found the Mid-American Conference Media Association, serving as its first president; was on the board of the Michigan Association Press Sports Editors Association; and was active with the Kalamazoo Center for Independent Living, Kalamazoo Wheelchair Athletic Association, the Optimists Club and the Elks Lodge.

Former *Gazette* publisher George Awady estimated that Jack wrote at least fifty-five thousand articles during his career, including columns featuring "This 'n' That," a positive line-up of notes and quips about locals, reminiscent of early twentieth-century social pages.

"He has written about more local people than anyone else ever has—and probably ever will," Awady wrote in 2002. "Year in and year out, Jack has written far more news articles and columns for the *Gazette* than any other writer." Jack outlasted every other *Gazette* employee, including four editors. It was the only job he ever held.

Retirement took Jack and his wife to Florida, where he continued to write articles and columns that appeared in the *Gazette*. He died on January 21, 2019, at the age of ninety-one, after a twenty-year battle with Parkinson's disease.

MARY "BONNIE" (GEORGE) BAKER

The nine children of Michael and Elizabeth (Lawrence) George grew up playing ball in their hometown of Regina in Saskatchewan, Canada, during the 1930s. Their daughter, Mary Geraldine, was the fourth oldest, born on June 10, 1918. She first took to the ballfield at the age of thirteen and also played basketball and participated in track in high school. After graduating in 1936, she married Maurice Griffith Baker.

Throughout the early years of her marriage, Mary played for three different softball leagues. While playing in a tournament in Chicago in 1939, a Scottish announcer called her a "bonnie lass," and from that point onward—at least on the field—she was known as Bonnie.

While Maurice served overseas during World War II, Mary earned fifteen dollars a week as a clerk in an army and navy store and was also catcher on the A&N Bombers softball team. It was during this time that she was invited to try out for the newly formed All-American Girls Professional Baseball League (AAGPBL, AAGPBL.org).

Fearing the war would pull men off the ballfields and onto the battlefields, Philip K. Wrigley, the chewing gum mogul and owner of the Chicago Cubs baseball franchise, led conversations to establish a girls' league to put fans in the stands. Nearly three hundred women participated in the spring training and selection camp on May 17, 1943, at Wrigley Field in Chicago. In the end, just sixty women were chosen to fill four teams of fifteen. Less than two weeks later, league play officially began on May 30. Players as young as fifteen were paid an average of $45 to $85 a week, while twenty-three-year-old Bonnie, the first Canadian to sign with the league, was offered an astounding $150 weekly.

For her first seven years, Bonnie (no. 12) was a catcher and infielder for the South Bend Blue Sox before transferring to Michigan to become a Lassie.

From the collection of Kalamazoo Valley Museum.

The expansion team started in Muskegon in 1946, but early in the 1950 season, with local support and finances drying up, the club moved to Kalamazoo. Bonnie, now sporting no. 7, played the infield and was also named team manager, the only woman to serve in such a capacity in the league's history and the first female manager in professional sports overall.

The Kalamazoo Lassies played at the lighted Lindstrom Field on the west side of Portage Street, just north of the intersection with Lovers Lane. Wearing the old Muskegon uniforms, as the new Kalamazoo ones weren't yet ready, Bonnie and her Lassies played 109 games that first year, winning just 36.

A pregnant Bonnie took the next season off (and welcomed her daughter Maureen, nicknamed Chick) but was back in Kalamazoo for her final season in 1952. After twelve years and with waning interest, the AAGPBL played its final games in 1954; the champions that year were the Kalamazoo Lassies.

Over her nine-year career, Bonnie played 930 regular season and 18 playoff games. She had a .965 fielding percentage, registered 225 RBIs, 506 stolen bases (including 94 in one season), 404 walks and struck out only 210 times. She played in 5 All-Star games, graced the pages of *SPORT* and *Life* magazines and appeared on the television show *What's My Line?* in 1950.

It is also commonly believed that it was Bonnie who inspired the character "Dottie Hinson," played by Geena Davis in the 1992 movie *A League of Their Own*. And like that character, Bonnie's sister, Genevieve "Gene" McFaul, was also a league player.

Back in Canada, Bonnie helped the Region Legion Club win the Women's Softball Championship in 1953, became Canada's first female sportscaster and, for twenty-five years, managed the Wheat City Curling Club. She was inducted into the Canadian Baseball Hall of Fame and Museum and the Saskatchewan Sports Hall of Fame. And after her death in 2003 at the age of eighty-four, she was honored with a mural in Regina's Central Park.

KEVIN VANDAM

Give a man a fish, and you feed him for a day; teach a man to fish and you feed him for a lifetime."

Kevin VanDam was born in Kalamazoo County (Alamo Township) on October 14, 1967, one of five children to Nadine (Sturman) and Dick VanDam. As a child, he loved spending time at his paternal grandparents' cottage on nearby School Section Lake in Bangor (Van Buren County). It was there, when he was about six years old, that he donned his first fishing suit, foreshadowing what was to come later in life.

When he was seven, Kevin joined his father and older brother Randy on a family fishing trip to Lake Leelanau northwest of Traverse City. It would become a monumental trip, as Kevin landed his first smallmouth bass, a twelve-incher, while drifting nightcrawlers over spawning beds from a fourteen-foot V-bottom boat, powered by a seven-and-a-half-horsepower Mercury outboard. That weekend, the young angler also caught fourteen-inch and eighteen-inch smallmouths, the largest among the group that weekend.

Back home, Kevin explored the trout streams near his home and learned to read the water and weather to improve his skills. Around the age of eleven, he transitioned from live bait to artificial lures on spinning rods, learning to maneuver many of the lures he still uses on School Section Lake.

As a teenager at Otsego High School (OHS), Kevin was involved in student council and played baseball until his senior year, when he decided spring fishing was more important to him than spring training. He was getting serious about fishing, and at the age of seventeen he won "Michigan Angler of the Year."

After graduating from OHS in 1985, Kevin focused most of his time and attention on competitive fishing, while working part time at a new tackle

KVD Outdoors.

shop that his brother and dad had recently started. D&R Sports Center (named for Dick and Randy) opened in 1982 across the parking lot from its current location at 8178 West Main Street (M-43). It added firearm and archery sales in 1986, and today, it's one of the largest hunting and fishing outfitters in the area, complete with boats, kayaks, marine products and accessories.

Kevin (known in the circuit as KVD) cast his line in professional fishing waters in 1990. Two years later, at the age of twenty-four, he became the youngest person to win the BASS Angler of the Year title. That was the first of seven he has since earned, in addition to one such title from the Fishing League Worldwide and eight from Major League Fishing (MLF). Over the last three-plus decades, he has competed in over 320 BASS events and owns 112 top-ten finishes, nearly 200 top-twenty finishes and 29 wins. He also has 4 Bassmaster Classic wins, 25 total BASS wins and 4 MLF Cup wins. Over his career, he racked up more than $7.2 million in winnings before retiring in 2023.

Considered the "Greatest Angler of All Time," Kevin was honored with the first-ever Outdoorsman of the Year ESPY Award by ESPN in 2002, was inducted into the OHS Hall of Fame in 2003 and, in 2018, was inducted into the Bass Fishing Hall of Fame (the same year he turned fifty).

The VanDams are angling royalty in Michigan and beyond. In addition to Kevin, Randy is a former State Champion Bass Angler, was the BASS Federation Angler of the Year in 1985 and, on June 16, 1993, caught Ohio's state record 9.8-pound smallmouth bass, a record that held for nearly thirty years until it was surpassed in the summer of 2022. Randy's son Jonathon (JVD) won his first BASS Elite Series Tournament in 2012. Kevin and his wife, Sherry, have twin boys named Jackson and Nicolas, who also enjoy fishing, although they're less competitive than their legendary father.

For more about Kevin, including information about the KVD Foundation, visit kevinvandam.com.

DEREK JETER

It is the American dream of so many young boys to become a professional baseball player. For one Kalamazoo kid, his relentless determination and hard work turned that dream into a major-league reality.

Dorothy Connors and Sanderson Charles Jeter met while they were both stationed with the army in Frankfurt, Germany, in 1972. Back in the United States, they lived briefly in Tennessee and were married the following year. Their son, Derek Sanderson Jeter, was born on June 26, 1974, in Pequannock Township, New Jersey, followed by their daughter, Sharlee, on November 20, 1979. Soon afterward, the family relocated to Kalamazoo, where Sanderson pursued a doctorate degree in psychology from Western Michigan University.

Derek learned the game of baseball firsthand at Oakwood Little League around the ages of seven or eight. It's likely his father had also regaled him with stories of his time playing shortstop for Fisk University in Nashville, Tennessee. According ESPN.com, when Derek was a fourth grader in Shirley Garzelloni's class at St. Augustine Cathedral School, he announced that he wanted to play shortstop for the New York Yankees. A few years later, he submitted an essay on the same topic in Chris Oosterbaan's eighth grade writing class. When Sally Padley, a British literature teacher at Kalamazoo Central High School, asked her students to create a personal coat of arms, Derek's featured a baseball player in a Yankee uniform swinging a bat.

Once Derek set his sights on this goal, he never wavered, and most of the decisions he made led him down a path toward his endgame. His supportive parents encouraged and challenged him, signing expectation contracts at the beginning of the school year to guide his classroom and extracurricular activities.

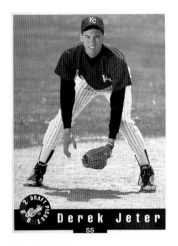

Classic Cards.

As a KC Maroon Giant, Derek played baseball and basketball and was a cross-country runner. He was president of the Latin Club, a member of the National Honor Society and graduated in 1992 with a 3.82 grade point average. During his senior year, he was named *USA Today's* High School Player of the Year, Gatorade High School Player of the Year, High School Player of the Year from the American Baseball Coaches Association, Kalamazoo Area B'nai B'rith Award for Scholar Athlete and earned a baseball scholarship to the University of Michigan. Yet before he could head off to Ann Arbor, the New York Yankees selected him with their sixth overall pick in the 1992 Major League Baseball draft.

For four years, Derek paid his dues in the minor leagues before donning the no. 2 and making his big-league debut on May 29, 1995, as a New York Yankee playing at the Kingdome, home of the Seattle Mariners. The Yankees lost (7–8), and Derek went hitless in five at bats, striking out once. It was a rough start, but Derek would go on to lead an impressive MLB career. He was named the American League Rookie of the Year in 1996, made fourteen All-Star appearances and landed in the top ten MVP voting eight times, winning it solo in 2000. In twenty seasons in the majors, Derek played only for his beloved Yankees, retiring in 2014. During his career, he was honored with five Gold Gloves, five Silver Sluggers and two Hank Aaron Awards as the American League's top hitter. In 2020, his first year of eligibility, he was elected to the Baseball Hall of Fame, receiving 396 of 397 possible votes, the second highest ranking in league history.

Derek is just as impressive off the field. In 1996, he and his father formed the Turn 2 Foundation (MLB.com/turn-2-foundation) to motivate young people to steer clear of drugs and alcohol by focusing on healthy lifestyle decisions, like participating in sports. His sister serves as the president of the organization. In November 2023, Derek was back in Kalamazoo to announce a $5 million project to renovate and reorient the baseball and softball diamonds at Kalamazoo Central, including new elevated aluminum grandstand seating, dugouts, synthetic turf and press boxes, as well as accessible bathrooms and parking.

SECTION 7
ENTERTAINERS AND BROADCASTERS

JOHN EARL FETZER

An early fascination with electronics, baseball, faith and spirituality led one ambitious man to follow his many dreams, leaving a resonating mark on history as well as a path toward future enlightenment.

John Earl Fetzer was born on March 25, 1901, in Decatur, Indiana, the first of two boys to Della Frances (Winger) and John Adam Fetzer. Della had two children from a previous marriage to David Edward Evans, who passed away in the 1890s. Just six weeks before young John's second birthday, his thirty-two-year-old father died of pneumonia. Shortly after that, Della moved with her children 120 miles away to Lafayette, Indiana.

Della remained a single mother until her third marriage to Irvin Ianthus Pyle in late 1917. When John was a child, his brother-in-law Frederick Lloyd Ribble (the first husband of his half-sister Harriet) introduced him to the world of radio, and the teenager soon built his first transmitter receiver. Frederick also cultivated John's love of baseball, specifically the Detroit Tigers, which became a personal passion John carried with him through life.

In 1922, John enrolled at Emmanuel Missionary College (now known as Andrews University), a Seventh-day Adventist College in Berrien Springs, Michigan, where he established its first radio station in 1923. He graduated in 1927 and, a few years later, purchased the underfunded radio station for $5,000 and moved it to Kalamazoo, the only major city in Michigan without its own radio station at the time. Set up inside the Burdick Hotel (located where the Radisson Plaza Hotel at Kalamazoo Center is now), WKZO became the foundation on which John's communications empire was built. The station (590 AM) still operates, now on West Main Street (M-43).

Over the years, John expanded his broadcast operations to include WKZO TV inside a remodeled car dealership at 590 West Maple Street in Kalamazoo (operating today as WWMT Channel 3). He set up shop in Grand

Fetzer Institute Archives (1923).

Rapids, Nebraska and Peoria, Illinois, under the umbrella Fetzer Company. He also founded Fetzer Music Corporation and Fetzer Cablevision, which became Charter Communications.

In 1956, John and a group of other individuals acquired the Detroit Tigers baseball team. By 1960, he had controlling interest in the club, and in 1961, he was the sole owner of the American League team, which went on to win the 1968 World Series. He later sold the team to Domino's Pizza mogul Tom Monaghan, remaining on as chairman of the board five years beyond the Tiger's 1984 World Series win, the same year he was inducted into the Michigan Sports Hall of Fame.

Another common theme throughout John's life was the connection he made between science and religion. His interest in parapsychology and spirituality surfaced through religious experiences he had during his childhood. He actively studied meditation, philosophy, prayer and the power of positive thinking. Later, through the Fetzer Institute, John's philanthropic contributions were directed toward supporting research-backed spiritual solutions to societal challenges. This included pioneering research that introduced mindfulness meditation into mainstream society.

The John E. Fetzer Foundation was established in 1954 to give grants for religious, charitable, scientific, library and educational purposes. He later set up operations in a triangular-shaped building—representing the mind, body and spirit—overlooking Dustin Lake on West KL Avenue in Oshtemo Township. The Fetzer Institute (Fetzer.org), whose mission is to help build the spiritual foundation for a loving world, was last valued at $732 million. John himself was ranked no. 239 on *Forbes* magazine's inaugural list of the "400 Wealthiest People in the United States" in 1982 (with a personal value of $125 million).

During his lifetime, John was a member at the local Presbyterian church and at a handful of local Masonic Lodge chapters, the Scottish Rite Valley (Northern Masonic Jurisdiction), Knights Templar and Saladin Shrine Temple. He died of pneumonia on February 20, 1991, in Honolulu, and was buried in Kalamazoo's Mountain Home Cemetery alongside his wife of sixty-two years, Rhea Y. Yeager (1901–1988).

PAUL HARVEY AURANDT

One of America's most iconic radio personalities, a man with a velvet voice that graced the airwaves for nearly six decades, spent part of his early career at WKZO radio in Kalamazoo.

A birth announcement in the *Sand Springs Leader* newspaper out of Tulsa, Oklahoma, read "a nine-pound boy arrived at the Harry H. Aurandt home in Tulsa Wednesday of last week. The Aurandts are well known to a number of our people." That boy was Paul Harvey Aurandt, born on September 4, 1918, to Anna Dagmar (Christensen) and Harry Harrison Aurandt.

When Paul was just two years old, his father, a Tulsa police officer, was murdered by robbers while off duty, leaving Anna to raise three children alone.

Paul developed an early interest in radio, picking up stations from a homemade cigar box crystal set. When he was a fourteen-year-old student at Tulsa Central High School, his teacher Isabelle Ronan nudged him toward a custodian job at radio station KVOO. He was soon filling in for on-air shifts, recording commercials and broadcasting the news. Paul continued at the station while attending the University of Tulsa, moving up the ranks to program director.

During the late 1930s, Paul was the operations director at WFBI in Kansas and then the director of news and special events at KOMA in Oklahoma City before moving on to KXOK in St. Louis, Missouri, in September 1938. While there, he met radio reporter Lynne Cooper, a graduate of Washington University.

Before they could marry, Paul boarded the steamship *Mastonia* in Los Angeles and arrived in Hawaii on Wednesday, March 13, 1940, for a three-month broadcasting stint. Less than ten days later, a brief in *The Honolulu Advertiser* announced that Paul had been added to the staff of station KGU.

WKZO Radio.

Paul and Lynne were eventually married on August 5, 1940, beginning a nearly seventy-year personal and professional partnership. That fall, Paul registered for the draft and later served in the U.S. Army Air Force, from December 1943 to March 1944, before being discharged for medical reasons.

The couple moved to Kalamazoo in 1941, when Paul was hired by WKZO radio as a program director and Lynne was hired as the director of women's activities and an educational advisor. In January 1942, Paul was named by the National Association of Broadcasters to serve as radio news chairman in Michigan and Indiana for the U.S. Office of War Information (OWI), while Lynne was chosen to represent Michigan and Indiana on the national committee of the Association of Women Broadcasters.

From Kalamazoo, the Aurandts moved to WENR in Chicago, where Paul dropped his surname and began opening his show with "Hello Americans, this is Paul Harvey," and closing with "Good day!" Within a year, his nightly broadcast became the top-rated program. It was here that Paul added his legendary "The Rest of the Story" segments, turning it into its own series on May 10, 1976. Broadcast until his death, it was one of the longest-running and most popular series in radio history, airing on more than 1,350 commercial radio stations, as well as 400 Armed Forces Radio Service stations, reaching a combined twenty-four million listeners.

During his esteemed fifty-seven-year career, Paul accumulated countless awards, including being inducted into the National Association of Broadcasters Radio Hall of Fame and being presented the Presidential Medal of Freedom from President George W. Bush.

Outside of the broadcasting world, Paul was an avid pilot and was a member of the Aircraft Owners and Pilots Association for more than fifty years. He was also a published author.

Lynne, whom Paul called "Angel," was considered the "First Lady of Radio" and was the first producer inducted into the NAB Hall of Fame. She died of leukemia in 2008. Paul died on February 28, 2009, at the age of ninety. Both were buried at Forest Home Cemetery Forest Park, Illinois. They are survived by their only child, Paul Harvey Jr.

MARY ALICE JACKSON

Growing up in a small town in Southeast Michigan was a recipe for success for a quiet and beautiful young woman who would go on to become a noted stage, television and film actress, including in a role on one of America's most beloved historical dramas.

Mary Alice Jackson was born on November 22, 1910, in Milford, Michigan (Oakland County) to Lela Vesta (Stephens) and Dr. Thomas Eugene Jackson. Her mother died when she was just eleven; her younger brother Ronald Earl would have been eight at the time.

It was about this time that Mary became interested in acting as she watched her classmates perform as part of the village's Monday Literary Club. Yet she kept her dreams to herself and never took to the stage until her senior year of high school.

Two years after graduating from Milford High School in 1927, a resourceful Mary had managed to save enough money to attend the Western State Teachers College in Kalamazoo. She had heard about an inspiring theater instructor, Laura Shaw, who had trained at the Moscow Art Theatre, and she desperately wanted to learn from her. Under Shaw's direction, Jackson was active in the Western State Players for at least two years.

According to her 1932 senior yearbook, Mary was cast in *The Dance Below* and, that same year, was noted as vice-president of the Players. During her time at Western State, she was also involved in forensics, serving as academy representative in 1931. This group participated in intramural debates and public speaking programs, which would have been useful tools for a woman interested in theater as a profession.

Early in her career, Mary made her way to stages in Detroit and Chicago before taking up a series of summer stock theaters. At one point, she joined a Shakespearean company and traveled throughout the United States,

Mary Jackson Collection at Milford Historical Society.

performing in a repertoire of fourteen plays, including shows at the Old Globe Theatre, a still-operating professional theater company located in Balboa Park in San Diego. She also performed in New York and Los Angeles with a list of shows to her credit.

It was 1952 before Mary made her first television and film appearances, cast on many well-known series like *The Twilight Zone*, *My Three Sons* and *Hazel*, among many others. She also had roles in several films, including *Airport*, *Audrey Rose*, *Big Top Pee-Wee* and *Leap of Faith*. Yet one role stood out above all the others.

The Waltons premiered at 8:00 p.m. on Thursday, September 14, 1972, on the CBS network, and it aired until June 4, 1981. Set in rural Virginia near the Blue Ridge Mountains during the Great Depression and on into the World War II era, the historical drama was based on the life of author Earl Hamner Jr.

Among the show's eccentric characters were privileged sisters Emily and Mamie Baldwin, played by Mary Jackson and Helen Kheeb, respectively. Living in their grand Victorian-era family home, these two spinster sisters (despite Emily's longing for her beau, Ashley Longworth Jr.) are best known for carrying on the family legacy as bootleggers, producing "the recipe" despite the illegalities of Prohibition. Mary reprised her role for all nine seasons (and 221 episodes) and for all the specials, the last being "A Walton Easter," which aired in 1997.

Mary often returned to Milford to visit classmates and friends. She was a charter member of the Milford Historical Society (MilfordHistory.org) and, in 1988, helped raise funds to rebuild the Oak Grove Cemetery Bridge over the Huron River, connecting the village to its oldest burial ground (where she and her family are interred). She owned two houses there, including the 1872 home where she was born.

Mary, who suffered from Parkinson's disease, died in Los Angeles on December 10, 2005, shortly after her ninety-fifth birthday. Upon her death, she willed the houses she owned in Milford to the historical society to operate as museums.

DARWIN BROWN

The ability to make someone smile and laugh is truly a gift. For more than a half century, one man made it his mission to deliver memories to children and families, no matter where his travels took him.

Darwin Elmer Brown was born on November 13, 1898, in Bloomingdale, Michigan, and was the adopted son of Delbert and Adah Ellen (Green) Brown. While his parents were farmers, Darwin felt a more public calling, one that would span decades and take him across the country to entertain crowds of all sizes.

An article in the September 22, 1971 issue of the *Kalamazoo Gazette* noted that the day before he married Opal Elizabeth Graves of Gobles (on December 20, 1919), he dressed up in costume for her second grade class and thus began his legendary career as Santa Claus.

But this wasn't the only character Darwin portrayed. In 1935, the *Kalamazoo Gazette* mentioned him performing as a "clowning cop" at a community celebration. A few years later, "Brownie the Clown," along with his trained donkey and dogs, began appearing at carnivals, festivals and county fairs throughout Michigan and the Great Lakes region. Over the years, he was active with the Shrine Circus and took up with traveling carnivals, variety shows and vaudeville acts that ventured from coast to coast.

The December 11, 1938, issue of the *Kalamazoo Gazette* featured one of the first published photographs of Darwin as Santa Claus, posed in a sleigh pulled by his donkey that was dressed as a reindeer. The article noted that he had publicly been playing Santa for the past six years (thirteen years after that first classroom appearance).

Sadly, in December 1941, Darwin's career nearly came to an end when he suffered a brain infection and had to undergo emergency surgery at Borgess Hospital (see pages 72–73). Despite reports that there was "little hope for

Darwin and Opal Brown (also known as Santa and Mrs. Claus) with the author and her older brother, Bob, around 1973. *Author's collection.*

recovery," he survived and was donning his holiday suit again for seasons to come.

Opal took great pride in making the costumes that she and Darwin wore, and they were so genuine looking that many considered the couple to be the "real" Santa and Mrs. Claus. Their shirts were made of white wedding satin, and with ten of them, Darwin was able to change during the day to keep himself looking fresh. He also wore black boots, a red hat with white fringe, white gloves and a red velvet suit to give himself a jolly appearance. His beard was crafted of imported yak hair, kept white from frequent washings and regular curling by his Mrs. Claus.

Over the years, Darwin made annual holiday visits to Borgess and Bronson Hospitals in Kalamazoo, as well Allegan Health Center and Lakeview Hospital in Paw Paw. He also made appearances at all the schools in Van Buren County and once even visited five in one night, to the enjoyment of children and their families. For years, Darwin and Opal were the highlight of the Kalamazoo Christmas parade.

Many from Kalamazoo and the surrounding communities may remember visiting Darwin and Opal each December at the Gilmore Brothers Department Store (see pages 100–101)—although it's likely only few knew their real names. They were simply known as Santa and Mrs. Claus, and for more than twenty years (starting in 1953), they listened to Christmas wishes and took photographs with tens of thousands of children.

In addition to portraying Brownie and Santa, Darwin was the voice of the Allegan County Fair. For nearly twenty-five years, his voice could be heard broadcast over the loudspeakers, sharing details about the day's schedule and other special attractions.

Darwin had a slight stroke in December 1976, which prevented him from playing Santa that season. It is unknown if he returned the following two years, but he died on February 11, 1978, at the age of seventy-nine. Opal passed away twenty years later, on April 23, 1998, at the age of ninety-seven. Both were buried in the Robinson Cemetery in Gobles.

JACK PEYTON AND BETTY RAGOTZY

A chance encounter on the stage at the Kalamazoo Civic Theatre, followed by a whirlwind courtship and a passion for acting were the foundation for a nearly fifty-year marriage and an iconic organization that has been going strong since 1946.

The February 1921 marriage between Louise (Gorden) and Floyd C. Ragotzy was short-lived, with their only child, Jack Peyton (born December 15, 1921), just a toddler when they divorced. Louise later married Meredith Fisher, and the family lived at 216 West Prouty Street in Kalamazoo.

Jack attended Kalamazoo Central High School on South Westnedge Avenue, where he discovered drama and honed his craft under the guidance of Howard M. Chenery, for whom Chenery Auditorium is named. He later joined the Kalamazoo Civic Players, both on and behind stage.

After graduating in 1937, Jack worked a series of jobs, and when Pearl Harbor was bombed on December 7, 1941, the twenty-year-old was at a recruiting station within forty-eight hours. He joined the U.S. Army Air Corps on August 21, 1942, remaining on reserve until the following February. He was sent to Texas as an aviation cadet, attending preflight school followed by bombardier and gunnery training. He earned his first wings that October as a second lieutenant in command of 160 men and served as a flight instructor. In his spare time, he directed the Midland Civic Theater in Texas.

Jack's first overseas assignment was on the island of Tinian for the 505th Bombardment Group, where he was involved in twenty-one missions over Japan. Staying on in Tinian for three months after the war, Jack passed the time building a theater and organizing a revue he called *Take It from Us*, which was performed in all eight island theaters.

The Barn Theatre School.

After being released from service as a first lieutenant on December 15, 1945, Jack returned home and enrolled at Kalamazoo College, where he studied literature, was a member of the College Players and French Club, took summer courses at nearby Western Teachers College and returned to the Kalamazoo Civic Stage.

The first show of the 1946 season was a comedy called *She Stoops to Conquer*, which opened on January 11 to rave reviews. Jack played Sir Charles, and twenty-three-year-old Betty Ebert was cast as the hostess's niece. Instantly smitten, the two were married less than a month later, on February 5, 1946.

A mutual love of theater led the newlyweds to establish the Village Players, operating out of the Richland Community Hall. Their first performance, *Charley's Aunt*, opened in July 1946. Finding the need for a more suitable venue, the Ragotzys rented an unused dairy barn on M-96 in Augusta that had been built six years earlier by Robert M. Cook. Jack and his crew raised the loft floor, built a stage and converted the stalls into dressing rooms, using $350 they pooled together. Tickets to the show cost $0.75 on Wednesday and Thursday nights and $0.90 on Fridays and Saturdays. During those early years, they barely made enough to pay the bills, but they happily returned the following season.

By 1954, the Ragotzys had purchased the barn as their permanent home, and today, it is regarded as Michigan's oldest resident summer stock theater and one of the few remaining equity companies in the country. Over the years, The Barn Theatre (BarnTheatreSchool.org) has hosted many well-known actors (affectionately called "Barnies"), like Jennifer Garner, Tom Wopat, Melissa Gilbert, Dana Delany, Robert Newman, Kim Zimmer, Scott Burkell and Joe Aiello, among many others. The theater was listed as a State of Michigan Historic site in 1983, receiving its marker in 1985.

Betty Ebert Ragotzy died on March 19, 1995, at the age of seventy-one. Jack passed away one day shy of his eighty-second birthday in 2003. Both were buried in the Augusta Cemetery. Their only child, Brendan, now runs the legendary theater with his wife, Penelope, and their four children.

REMBERT "REM" WALL

A small-town midwestern boy—a coal miner's son—spent his early years singing in the church choir and listening to legendary country music performers on the family radio, dreaming of becoming a star himself someday.

Rembert "Rem" Wall was born on October 2, 1918, on a farm outside West Frankfort, Illinois (situated between St. Louis, Missouri, and Nashville, Tennessee), one of three children and the only son of Scott "McKinley" and Jennetta "Jennie" (Neal) Wall.

As a child, Rem sang in the church choir and took gospel-singing lessons, the only formal music training he ever had. He listened to country music records and tuned in each week to hear iconic figures like Ernest Tubb, Red Foley and others sing on WSM radio. Around the age of twelve, Rem taught himself to yodel and play a Kalamazoo-made Gibson guitar that was gifted to him by an uncle. In high school, he was a member of The Boys of the Golden West, and as a young man, he was known as the "Yodelin' Romeo" on the *Hayloft HiJinks* show on WEBQ out of Harrisburg, Illinois.

In 1939, Rem's fiancée, Roberta Black, moved to Kalamazoo for a nursing job at Bronson Methodist Hospital, and Rem soon followed. The couple was married on September 27, 1941, and they would go on to have three children: Rendal in 1942, Rebecca in 1947 and Rodney in 1951.

Once in Kalamazoo, Rem took a job with the Gibson Mandolin-Guitar Manufacturing Company (see pages 34–35), where he stayed for nearly four decades (with a brief hiatus in employment in his early years there). During World War II, he was a vocalist with Ma Brumfield and Her Kentucky Hill Billies, playing frequently for the soldiers stationed at Fort Custer in nearby Augusta.

In the mid-1940s, Rem began performing regularly on Carl Collins's farm program on WKZO radio (see pages 118–119), and after that, he had his

Fetzer Institute Archives.

own weekly show on Saturday nights with The Green Valley Boys. He later worked as a DJ at WGFG (now WKMI), where he had the opportunity to interview Roy Rogers and Dale Evans in studio.

Rem made the jump to WKZO TV when *The Green Valley Jamboree* program debuted on January 15, 1954. The show ran live every Friday night through 1975, when it became a prerecorded program (to accommodate sports broadcasts), airing until November 29, 1980. At the time, it was the longest-running country music TV show in history.

In 1959, Rem performed at the legendary Buck Lake Ranch in Angola, Indiana, with his musical hero Ernest Tubb. That year, he also represented American country music in a Kalamazoo exhibit at the Berlin Industrial Fair in Germany and signed a six-year, seven-album recording contract with Columbia Records. In 1963, he wowed the crowd at the Disc Jockey Convention, later performed on the Grand Ole Opry stage at the Ryman Auditorium and, in 1977, was inducted into the Michigan Country Music Hall of Fame.

Throughout the years, Rem's children all performed at various times with the band. In his final years, Rem could be found entertaining residents at local nursing homes through Renaissance Enterprises with fellow musician Bob Rowe, who was just eighteen the first time he performed on *The Green Valley Jamboree*.

"He was my hero then, and just about the biggest country star around, in my eyes," Bob recounts. "He was on TV for thirty years, longer than I'd been alive. Every Saturday night, my brothers and sisters and I, Mom and Dad and Grandma, sat around the television set to hear Rem and The Green Valley Boys sing their hearts out, especially the hymns and standards.... They were my favorites."

On August 15, 1994, Rem underwent open heart surgery, but just a few weeks later, on September 4, he passed away at the age of seventy-five due to complications from diabetes. He was buried in Mount Ever-Rest Memorial Park South in Kalamazoo, alongside Roberta, who passed away in 1978 from multiple sclerosis.

MYRON EUGENE "GENE" RHODES

Each fall, families from all around Southwest Michigan make a pilgrimage to 22637 M-43 Highway West in search of autumn décor—most notably, the perfect pumpkin, proudly grown by one of the community's most colorful characters and third-generation farmers.

Myron Henry Rhodes purchased forty fertile acres just west of the Kalamazoo and Van Buren County line in Section 13 of Almena Township from A. Todd (likely Albert May Todd, see pages 42–43) on May 5, 1885, and set out to establish a family farm with his wife, Mattie E. (Deal). A cooper by trade, Myron made barrels in South Haven during the winter, traveling to the lakeshore by train from Williams Crossing some five miles from the farm. In the summer, he planted and harvested wheat, hay, corn and some vine crops (in an area later known as one of Michigan's prime vineyard regions). He also raised an assortment of farm animals—cows, horses, pigs, sheep and chickens, among others.

In 1906, Myron undertook the massive job of moving his barn to its present location on M-43 Highway using a team of horses and lots of manual labor. Given the increased amount of traffic along this trunkline, he was often called on to help travelers repair their buggy or wagon wheels. He was prone to serve up a meal to hungry beggars or assist a weary passerby in other ways.

Myron was also the director of the one-room District 7 Moore School on nearby Fish Hatchery Road in the late 1890s, where his six children were students. This included his fourth child, Ralph Deal, who had been born on Easter Sunday, April 14, 1895, in the original farmhouse (razed in 1972). Ralph took over the family business in 1925, after his father's death, while also clocking in more than thirty years as a conservation officer at the nearby Wolf Lake State Fish Hatchery.

Gene the Pumpkin Man.

Ralph and his wife, Evelyn M. (Harris), welcomed their son, Myron Eugene Rhodes, known today as "Gene the Pumpkin Man," during a snowstorm on Tuesday, February 11, 1936, at 7:30 a.m. As a child, Gene also attended the Moore School (where his father was also serving as director) and worked on the farm, feeding the animals, cleaning stalls and selling sweet corn from a roadside stand. Later, he walked behind his father as he plowed the field with a team of horses. While a student at Mattawan High School, Gene was a member of the Future Farmers of America (FFA) and performed in both his junior and senior plays, landing the male lead in *Hillbilly Weddin'* during his senior year before graduating in 1954.

In 1957, the family began planting pumpkins and growing their legacy, as denoted in large black letters on the historic orange barn (which still stands). Today, Gene sells about two hundred tons of pumpkins, as well as gourds, straw, mums, pumpkin butter and honey.

"Dad lived all his life on the farm until a few months before he died in 1977," Gene wrote in an historic booklet on file at the Kalamazoo Public Library. "The farm and heritage which it represents was then passed on to me to continue the tradition. I may not have been born on the farm, but I have not lived anywhere else. My roots go very deep."

Outside of the farm, Gene worked twenty-seven years for the Michigan Commission for the Blind, retiring in 1997. Prior to that, he worked ten years for the TB Sanatorium and four years at Kendall Industrial Hardware Store. In addition to his thriving pumpkin empire, this local legend—always clad in his signature orange—is a longstanding president of the West Oshtemo Grange Association (a local fraternal farmers' organization founded in 1917) and a member of both the Michigan Farm Bureau and West Oshtemo Baptist Church (where, in 1954, he was noted as a junior deacon and, in 1960, was chairman of the board of deacons).

NARADA MICHAEL WALDEN

One of America's most celebrated music producers started playing drums as a child in Kalamazoo dive bars and later led his high school marching band before following his dreams to California.

Michael Walden was born on April 23, 1952, in Plainwell, the oldest of six children of Marguerite "Peggy" Estelle (Hackley) and Harold Walden. His love of music came at an early age when his grandfather Valentine D. Hackley bought him his first real drum set—a Ludwig snare, bass and cymbal—setting in motion a career that has spanned six decades (and counting).

Tom Carey was Walden's first drum teacher, followed by the "Godfather of Jazz" Bobby Davidson, who owned Davidson's Music Shoppe on the Kalamazoo Mall, was on the music faculty at Western Michigan University (WMU) and was leader/drummer of the Bobby Davidson Orchestra. Another early mentor was Harold Mason, who went on to play drums with Michigan's own Stevie Wonder, one of Walden's early influences. At the age of eleven, the budding drummer formed a band called The Ambassadors, with Joel Brooks on organ, opening for headliners at the Ambassador Lounge on Patterson Street in Kalamazoo.

Marching and symphonic bands (under director Don Agne) were added to Walden's repertoire during his years at Plainwell High School (PHS). As a junior, he went to camp to learn the signals, calls, baton and whistle action to become the drum major of the Trojan Marching Band, a position he held for his last two years of high school. While at PHS, he was also active in forensics and the Pep and Drama Clubs and was voted the most popular, best dressed and most creative graduate of the class of 1970.

A Martin Luther King Jr. scholarship landed Walden at WMU, where he studied music, played in the jazz band and even participated in the summer

Grand Marshal Narada Michael Walden with the author at the 1987 Wine and Harvest Festival parade. *Author's collection.*

music program. While there, he was part of a couple of rock bands, including Distance in the Far and Avatar, playing hole-in-the-wall bars around the state and perfecting his craft.

College provided Walden with musical theory, but it didn't give him the hands-on performing time he desired. After his third-semester exams were over, he happened to check out a local show with Deacon Williams and the Soul Revival and was drawn in by their funk sound. Since they needed a drummer and he was looking to spread his wings, he jumped on the bus and traveled with the band to Fresno, California. That gig was short-lived, and Walden relocated to Miami to join the New McGuire Sisters, a jazz/rock band inspired by John McLaughlin's Mahavishnu Orchestra, a group he ultimately joined in 1973. In the 1970s, he also took up meditation and followed the teachings of Indian guru Sri Chimoy, adding Narada, meaning "supreme musician," to his name.

In the 1980s, Narada skyrocketed to the top of the class as an A-list producer at Tarpan Studios (Tarpanstudios.com), which he founded in 1985 in San Rafael, California. With a client list that included the hottest entertainers of the time—Diana Ross, Lionel Ritchie, Barbra Streisand, Hall and Oates, Starship, Mariah Carey, Elton John, Sting, George Michael and many others—Narada made his mark on the music industry. He earned a Grammy in 1985 for Aretha Franklin's "Freeway of Love," and two years later, he was named Producer of the Year. His longstanding relationship with Whitney Houston is well documented, and in 1993, they won Album of the Year for *The Bodyguard: The Original Soundtrack Album*, which sold over 15 million copies. He also released several albums under his own name, including the latest called *Euphoria*.

Kalamazoo still holds a special place in Narada's heart. In 1987, he served as the grand marshal of the Wine and Harvest Festival Parade and even produced a music video called "Christmas Time in Candy Cane Park" based on the city's annual holiday display in Bronson Park.

JAMES HIGGS

A childhood love of radio led to a long-standing career spanning seven decades, as well as a place in rock-and-roll history.

The only child of Robert and Ruth (Walker) Higgs, James Robert was born in Plainwell on October 9, 1964. He was in the first class at the current Gilkey Elementary School, and in high school, he was involved in the Latin Club, student council, band and junior and senior plays, graduating in 1962.

That August, Jim entered a twelve-by-sixty-foot trailer (marked with the letters WDMC-AM980) near the Kalamazoo River, west of Otsego, for a job interview. His brief audition must have impressed the owners because the next day, Jim was on the air. That stint was brief, and the following summer, he accepted an announcer position with WHTC-AM/FM in Holland. After four years, in April 1967, Jim made the move to WKMI in Kalamazoo, serving in multiple roles, including news director, program director, music director and on-air personality for the morning drive shift.

In the early 1970s, Jim helped an up-and-coming band make music history. In August 1974, Elektra-Asylum released the single "James Dean," from the Eagles' third album, *On the Border*. The band, which formed in 1971, had earned a few Top 10 hits but hadn't yet reached stardom. While the label was aggressively pushing "James Dean," Jim chose to play a ballad written by Don Henley, Glenn Frey and J.D. Souther. The song became an instant hit in the Kalamazoo market, and local record stores couldn't keep the album or 45 RPM in stock.

While "James Dean" struggled (never ranking higher than 77 on the charts), Jim was trying to convince executives to release that ballad as a single. Finally, on November 5, 1974, it was released nationally and flew up the Billboard Hot 100 charts. By March 1975, the Eagles had landed their first no. 1 single: "Best of My Love." Later that year, Burt Stein

Left: *Jim Higgs Collection.*

Below: Rip Pelley (*left*) and Burt Stein (*right*) of Elektra-Asylum present Jim Higgs (*center*) with an autographed copy of the Eagles' *On the Border* album in 1975. *Jim Higgs Collection.*

Top: Jim Higgs and with members of the Eagles (*left to right*: Timothy B. Schmit, Glenn Frey, Joe Walsh and Don Henley) backstage at Van Andel Arena in Grand Rapids, Michigan, on September 8, 2014. *Author's collection.*

Bottom: Jim Higgs and his family with members of the Eagles backstage at Van Andel Arena in Grand Rapids, Michigan, on September 8, 2014. *Left to right*: Caleb Stampfler, Timothy B. Schmit, Glenn Frey, Mollie Stampfler, Jim Higgs, Suzanne Higgs, Don Henley, Joe Walsh, Dianna Higgs Stampfler and Justin Shemberger. *Author's collection.*

and Rip Pelley, representatives from Elektra-Asylum, presented Jim with a framed, band autographed copy of the album cover, which hung in his office for years.

Following thirteen years at WKMI, Jim moved to WNWN—Stereo Country 98 as a DJ and later as program director. In 1983, he joined forces with several other local radio industry leaders to buy WAOP AM/FM in Otsego (formerly WDMC, the station where he had started twenty years earlier). The station soon became WQXC (Quixie), and the group purchased other stations, including WBNZ in Benzonia and WSTR in Sturgis. While there, Jim jumped back into the morning drive seat, while also serving as program director. By 1993, the corporation that owned Quixie (now Cool 101) had dissolved, and Jim took ownership of the AM station, WAKV AM 980, running it from a studio in the basement of his house (the family home where his mother had grown up). He officially retired from the radio business in February 2021 after fifty-nine years on air.

The story about the Eagles' first no. 1 single was a family favorite, and it became public in September 2014, when the band performed at Van Andel Arena in Grand Rapids. Jim, who hadn't attended a concert in more than thirty years, was invited backstage with his family to meet the band. Later, during their performance of "Best of My Love," the band publicly thanked Jim from the stage and later recounted the story in various media interviews—including one in *Rolling Stone*.

An avid genealogist and historian, Jim was the second of soon-to-be five generations to attend Plainwell Community Schools. Over the years, he was active in various aspects of government with the City of Plainwell, including serving six years as mayor and terms on the planning commission, library board and airport board. In September 2024, city leaders dedicated the James R. Higgs Industrial Park in honor of his years of service to his hometown.

Jim passed away on May 5, 2024, at his family home in Plainwell, five months shy of his eightieth birthday.

AUTHOR'S NOTE

This manuscript is a compilation of historical dates and other information from a variety of sources, including firsthand accounts. While the details are not always consistent, what is printed here represents an honest attempt to relay the facts or accounts as accurately as possible.

ABOUT THE AUTHOR

Dianna Higgs Stampfler has been writing professionally since her junior year at Plainwell High School when she was also a reporter for the local weekly newspaper. By her senior year, she had her own column in that paper, was serving as news editor of her award-winning school newspaper and was also working in the newsroom at a local radio station (following in the footsteps of her father, who was a DJ for nearly sixty years before retiring in 2021; see pages 134–137).

She graduated from Western Michigan University with a dual degree in English with an emphasis in community journalism and communications with an emphasis in broadcasting. Dianna went on to work in public relations at Otsego Public Schools, where she also launched a middle school and elementary student newspaper program. Within four years, she was advising one of the top middle school newspapers in the state of Michigan, until she was forced out following a highly publicized case involving First Amendment issues and her student journalists.

In 1997, Dianna began working in Michigan's tourism industry, promoting destinations within a forty-one-county region at the West Michigan Tourist Association. In 2004, she launched Promote Michigan (PromoteMichigan. com), a public relations consulting company specializing in the hospitality, tourism, agriculture, culinary natural resources, recreation, history and culture industries. It is her lifelong passion to share the stories of the people, places and products of Michigan and the Great Lakes region.

Over the past three decades, Dianna has penned countless articles for publications such as *Michigan Blue* magazine, *Lakeland Boating*, *Michigan Meetings & Events* magazine, *West Michigan Carefree Travel*, *SEEN* magazine, *Michigan Home & Lifestyle*, *Pure Michigan Travel Ideas*, *Rural Innovation Exchange*, *UPword* and countless others.

In 2019, Dianna's first book, *Michigan's Haunted Lighthouses*, was published by The History Press and made it to number 2 on Amazon for haunted titles. It was later adapted for young readers as part of The History Press's Spooky America series. Her second book, *Death & Lighthouses on the Great Lakes: A History of Murder & Misfortune*, was published by The History Press in 2022 and blends her passions for maritime history, dark tourism and true crime.

Visit us at
www.historypress.com